POWER VISION
How to Unlock the Six Dimensions of Executive Potential

George W. Watts

BUSINESS ONE IRWIN
Homewood, Illinois 60430

This publication is designed to provide accurate and authoritative information in regard to the subject matter covered. It is sold with the understanding that neither the author nor the publisher is engaged in rendering legal, accounting, or other professional services. If legal advice or other expert assistance is required, the services of a competent professional person should be sought.

From a Declaration of Principles jointly adopted by a Committee of the American Bar Association and a Committee of Publishers.

Sponsoring editor:	Cynthia A. Zigmund
Project editor:	Rebecca Dodson
Production manager:	Mary Jo Parke
Designer:	Laurie Entringer
Compositor:	Publishing Resource Group
Typeface:	11/13 Palatino
Printer:	The Book Press, Inc.

Library of Congress Cataloging-in-Publication Data

Watts, George W.
Power vision: how to unlock the six dimensions of executive potential / George W. Watts.
p. cm.
ISBN 1-55623-808-8
1. Executive ability. I. Title.
HD38.2.W38 1993
658.4'09—dc20 92-25000

Printed in the United States of America

1 2 3 4 5 6 7 8 9 0 BP 9 8 7 6 5 4 3 2

This book is dedicated to my parents, George and Suzanne Watts—they taught me to seek vision.

To my wife, Mary Beth, my brother Cameron, and my daughters: Christen, Shawna, Remember, and India.

Acknowledgments

For all they have done and will do: George Haworth, Mark Allyn, and Don Ellison.

Many executives have greatly contributed to my understanding of human behavior. Sincere thanks to them all. I'd like to express my special appreciation to the following friends and clients: Ken Harz, Arthur von Rosenburg, Mary Lynn Bryden, Herb Carrel, Brenda Beckham, John Drought, Guy Chipman, Dennis O'Malley, Gay Meyer, Tom Higgins, Tony Anderson, John Lewis, Rita Testo DiAgostino, John Peveto, John Matthews, Larry Kane, Dan Weinfurter, Walter Ross, Jack Koon, Alex Halff, and Jim Kucera.

This book was made possible through the efforts of these extraordinary individuals for supporting this project. For reading my manuscript and making that special phone call—Cindy Zigmund, my editor, and all the talented folks at Business One Irwin.

For her dedication, editing, creativity, and encouragement—Susan Price.

For his careful eye and wonderful daughter—Col. William J. Cavoli (ret.).

And for my friend who supports me and has always believed. Words can never express my thanks to my partner, Kathy Rubin. With her loving patience and endurance she cajoled, prodded and at times, demanded that I write this book. She was enormously helpful in editing and design as well.

Contents

Introduction

Business desperately needs men and women with the courage and determination to create a vision and to bring that vision into reality in a team-oriented environment. But how do executives and managers visualize their highest potential and put ego needs aside in order to work with and through others? What is the progression from management "techniques" to developing a strategy that utilizes and maximizes the highest energy of the individual and the team?

Power Vision—How to Unlock the Six Dimensions of Executive Potential lays the framework for the thoughtful reader to achieve full integration of all of his or her strengthswith the team. A psychiatrist, Dr. Carl Gustav Jung, introduced the term *individuation* to describe the mature person whose potentials are fulfilled and whose self-realization is attained.

This book is for people who wish to expand their knowledge of self, their ability to be a better leader and a follower, to communicate with clarity and respect, in order to become a valuable member of a team that energies and motivates their organization.

The first chapter, "Power Insight," begins the most important task of the individuation process—the acquisition of self-knowledge. This is continuous throughout the lifespan. Without honest self-appraisal, managers are empty shells with no real substance of their own. Without a continuous process of self-understanding, people become too one-sided in their outlooks. This narrowness leads to rigidity, and is the essence of poor managerial style.

The personality we show to others is only a mask we wear. Most often, we believe that there is nothing more to personality than social roles. Although our masks are necessary to live together effectively, the most important parts of our personality are the ongoing conscious acknowledgment of truth when we perceive it and our unconscious, the part of our minds we are not aware of. This is where our behavior emanates from, and where the challenges of personal growth lie. We are all aware of some of our faults, but many others are kept out of our awareness, in the realm of the unconscious. We must explore the undesirable aspects of ourselves. We cannot become individuated persons unless we learn about these hidden elements.

The second chapter, "Power Growth," continues this train of thought by tracing the development of maturity. Through balancing the feminine and masculine aspects within each of us, we expand our personalities and increase our personal awareness. The social persona no longer controls our behavior and is not the center of the personality. There is freedom, and talents are allowed to be expressed. Executives can use their roles to inflate their egos by the attributes of their status, but they suffer the consequences of this falseness. A balanced individual makes for an effective executive. Managerial ability and growth occur naturally, but the superior executives deliberately work to express and improve the traits they were given.

Chapter three, "Power Intuition," advocates that the mature executive, with experience, begins to believe in his or her intuition. The philosophy of intuition is examined, as well as how to enhance your intuition in business decision making. Decision-making confidence is a function of how well your rational mind correlates with your intuitive mind. Executives eventually learn to obey their feelings they consider unbiased and thus inherently and spontaneously understand what is to be done. With intuition, executives learn to be multidimensional.

Chapter four, "Power Leaders," deals with fusing your head with your heart in cementing your leadership style. There is a balance between spontaneous, emotional decision making and playing it so safe by the numbers that action isn't taken in time. Balance fuses the head and the heart—the rational and emotional. Without this balance, illusion occurs. Through analogy and example, it is shown that the highest-functioning executives recognize and appreciate how this balance creates a better leader. The emerging new roles of the modern-day executive are also touched upon.

Chapter five, "Power Teams," makes the point that a company's true value is in the quality of its team consciousness. The team leader serves as a role model to show employees how to be successful. He or she must teach and live ego restraint, help the team not to fear the unknown, deal with conflict, and realize that all people want more freedom to do their jobs. Good leaders create a sense of excitement, urgency and inspiration. This pivital chapter pulls together the concepts of self knowledge, leadership and communication, and takes these concepts from the individual to the group.

The sixth chapter, "Power Communication," shows how to promote yourself while fulfilling the needs of those around you. This is the essence of leadership. Present-day executives realize the world is enormously complicated and at best they only understand a tiny fraction of it. In order to manifest their destiny, they must create a climate of motivation and engender the support and knowledge of those who surround them. Interpersonal communication skills inform the readers of positive, relatively easily grasped principles that can aid them in fostering the synergistic relationships they need in order for them and their companies to become even more successful.

Seminars based on the concepts in POWER VISION are available. These unique and motivating programs are specifically designed to energize the management team in order to energize their bottom line.

Public seminars are also available. For more information on both in-house and public seminars, please call Executive Visions at 1-800-626-4361.

Chapter 1

Power Insight

At the heart of the truly advanced, mature executive is self-knowledge. Only through knowing yourself can you grow and achieve. Personal growth through understanding and self-analysis is your responsibility—yours alone. No one else can do this for you.

Professional mental health workers discover in the early stages of their training that they must understand *themselves* before they are allowed to help others. Future psychiatrists undergo complete analysis before being allowed to analyze others. Most counseling and psychology degree programs demand that candidates undergo a complete battery of tests and personal counseling to help them resolve any problems they may have that would impact their ability to work with others.

Self-knowledge is the most effective approach to developing yourself as an executive. It is the *only* approach that will bring you lasting success. Understanding yourself also carries some great side effects: inner peace, an open mind, a less judgmental attitude, and greater self-esteem.

An old joke among industrial psychologists is that one executive has 20 years of experience, and another executive has one year of experience 20 times. The difference between the two is self-assessment and introspection. Blind spots are limiting. Despite evidence of job success, when an executive's weaknesses have not been recognized and an attempt made to resolve them, the executive has not grown.

Executives with intellectual knowledge are an abundant resource in the working world. Wisdom, a much rarer commodity, comes to those few people who are mature enough to view themselves realistically. Society needs more mature executives, not more knowledgeable ones. There are many people in business with excellent recall and understanding of their fields. These skills are useless without the higher skills of synthesis, creativity, and maturity.

LOOK AT YOURSELF HONESTLY

You begin to understand yourself through truthful internal communication. The better you internally communicate, the better you can externally communicate. When you understand yourself and are honest with yourself, you can more honestly relate to others. Strive to think the truth about yourself. Don't picture yourself as you want others to see you. Examine yourself with a mirror that reflects your *true* appearance.

Powerful, wealthy, and successful people often have big egos and do not look at their inner selves. They only consider the persona they want other people to see. They don't engage in introspection. *Introspection* is a term that mental health professionals use to describe the process of looking within. Through introspection, we learn what is the truth *for us*. Reality for you is not reality for someone else.

Through reading this book, you are demonstrating a willingness to engage in introspection. You have begun the process of discovering what is the truth for you. As a result, when you listen to another person, you will understand immediately whether that person is speaking truth to you. Let me illustrate.

If I, as a consultant, tell you that you are a very able administrator but that you will have trouble in sales because you are sensitive to rejection, you grasp intuitively—immediately—if those words are true for you. If you know yourself well and know you are sensitive, you have likely steered clear of the sales arena for that reason. On the other hand, if I tell you that you are doomed because you don't share my religious beliefs, you may or may not accept my statement as being true for you.

We know the truth about ourselves when we hear it. But if we have solid self-esteem, we discard other people's truths as we see fit. Being honest with yourself leads you to insights and growth. Generally, at a certain point, an "inner knowing" dominates. Inner knowing occurs when you understand truth as it applies to you. The journey of self-knowledge is a long and sometimes painful process. With patience and resolve, you will grow and benefit from the power of your effort. The knowledge of self is permanent. Once you begin to understand, you can never "unknow" yourself.

KNOW YOUR WEAKNESSES AND STRENGTHS

Know your limitations, but don't let this knowledge handicap you. Knowing, understanding, and coming to grips with your limitations and weaknesses doesn't indicate poor self-esteem —it demonstrates strong self-confidence. A sure sign of your psychological strength is the accurate acknowledgment of your weaknesses. Only by understanding your weaknesses can you strive to overcome them. Only by overcoming your weaknesses can you change, grow, and evolve.

As a consultant, I frequently see executives who hang onto the personality and knowledge that helped them early in their careers. It is difficult for them to discard traits and beliefs they feel have been helpful to them. But as your responsibility level grows and changes, so must your skills grow and change. The theories, ideas, and beliefs that may have helped you in the past must be discarded in favor of creating a new you. You must constantly alter your personality traits to develop new and better ones.

Have an open mind. Don't condemn or judge yourself; this makes you reluctant to look at yourself at all. Human beings have a natural tendency to see the negative and then judge that negative. Begin to understand yourself by simply analyzing and studying your daily conduct or thoughts for meanings and symbols.

An executive I know agonized over his decision to buy an expensive Mont Blanc fountain pen. He went to great lengths to justify in his mind how smoothly the pen would write, and how much better his writing—particularly his signature—would look. He finally went out and bought one.

I pointed out to him that this pen was a symbol of success in his mind. He thought about it, and somewhat sheepishly agreed. That simple insight gave him some food for thought. He craved status, and that need for status covered up some feelings of poor self-esteem.

At night, take some time to understand the real meaning behind the day's actions. Make it part of your nightly ritual. Assess yourself by questioning the type of energy you used today. What were your true motives?

Some people have found keeping a diary of their behavior for a week or two to be particularly enlightening. One friend of mine found that she spent much of the day being judgmental and making sarcastic remarks. Until she examined the evidence of her own behavior, she thought of herself as friendly and outgoing.

These honest self-assessments in the evening can be humbling, but this is encouraging—it means you're doing it right. Only through understanding your weaknesses can you overcome them.

We have all seen examples of people with physical problems overcome and rise above their problems. I was afflicted with a speech disorder as a child. Through patience, love, willpower, and the help of a therapist, I overcame those problems. Today I am a public speaker. When I really look at that speech impediment, I realize it was a blessing in disguise. Overcoming it gave me the confidence and direction to help me find my career.

As you strive to understand yourself, think about your positive attributes and abilities as well. All of us possess some outstanding characteristics; some even have true signs of genius. Use this understanding of your strengths to place yourself into a position which utilizes these strengths. Are you particularly well organized? Then get into a position that requires good organizational skills. If you are introverted, look for a position in which you can analyze information by yourself. If you are extroverted, get into a people-intensive role where you solve problems, integrate work teams, and deal with the public.

As a management consultant, I evaluate candidates for top executive positions with interviews and personality and ability tests. I try to determine whether the candidate sitting across from me is capable of performing the job my client company has available. Invariably, the executives I recommend for top jobs are psychologically mature. In fact, over the years, I've become convinced that psychological maturity and intelligence are the two *key* components needed for effective executive functioning.

In my interview, I always ask job candidates to describe their strengths and weaknesses. The mature candidates analyze themselves very well; their self-analysis tends to match what I find out about them through personality testing and interviewing. The poorer candidates try to inflate their abilities. When asked to describe their weaknesses, they respond poorly. It is obvious to me that they have not undergone introspection, and are hence unable to describe themselves very well. They give superficial, noninsightful responses which reveal to me that these candidates have not thought deeply about themselves. As a consequence, they have blind areas that impact their judgment. If the job requires accurate judgment—and executive jobs do—such a candidate is not right for the job.

Weaker job candidates have no problem talking about their strengths. In fact, it's hard to get them to shut up. But when probed for weaknesses, they give noninsightful responses such as "I work too hard," or "I expect too much of my people because I expect so much of myself." About 50 percent of the time, I hear the old standby, "problems with time management." In contrast, the outstanding executives admit in the interview that sometimes they are overly sensitive to criticism, or that they would like to have better control of their emotions.

LOOK AT PEOPLE YOU DISLIKE

Another way to understand yourself is to look at the people you dislike. There are probably very few people whom you genuinely dislike. There are probably lots of people you don't care to be around for any length of time, but as long as they stay in their space and you stay in yours, you can be cordial. Look at the people you genuinely dislike for some reason. What is it about them—specifically—that you dislike? Upon closer inspection of these people, you may discover some facet in them that brings forward and makes known to you a weakness that you have. Their personality reminds you of your weakness, and because of that recognition, you dislike them.

For example, perhaps you don't like someone you consider self-centered. When you examine that person more deeply, you find that he or she intimidates you, and you give in. When you examine yourself further, you find that dominant people in general take advantage of you. Assertiveness is difficult because of a low level of self-esteem that you can't admit to yourself.

During my tenure as a corporate executive, an authoritarian, opinionated, ex-military member of the management team had an office across the hall from mine. I disliked him intensely. In conversation one day he revealed to me, "I don't care if anybody likes me or not. Being liked isn't important to me."

I was repelled by his statement. I couldn't imagine anybody approaching the world with that attitude. Upon greater reflection, however, I realized that some of my dislike for that viewpoint stemmed from the fact that I had a very *high* need to be liked. A high need to be liked is a weakness in an executive. It makes it more difficult to perform some executive tasks. This insight helped my career immensely.

TEST YOURSELF

Another way to understand yourself is to take personality tests. Personality tests measure various aspects of your personality. Traits that are measured by testing include dominance, enthusiasm, extroversion, self-confidence, self-discipline, and the like. Executives will sometimes tell me, "I don't believe in those tests." Most of the time, this is because they have a fear of being exposed; they are concerned about the results. It seems that the top executives *like* to take personality tests, and have taken many of them throughout the course of their lives. They know themselves well but are always willing to learn more and grow as a result. The more afraid and nervous you are about personality tests, the greater your lack of self-insight.

I use personality testing to help executives understand who they really are. Occasionally, the president of one of my client companies wants me to interview and test the members of his entire executive team. It's my policy to do this only if the individual team members are willing. Invariably, domineering and authoritarian executives are highly resistant to working with me. They feel the tests don't mean anything, and that it's a ridiculous way to spend money. Inwardly, they feel threatened, insecure, and exposed.

Some of them are very clever in their innovative ways to avoid me. They never seem to have time to set up their appointment for me to interview them, and they drag out the process for as long as they can. One executive had to go to Europe for six weeks—exactly the duration of the consulting. I remember another one breaking six appointments. Anything they could do to avoid me, they did. Authoritarians don't like personality testing.

Personality tests aren't perfect, but they are good indicators. They can give you some information. Most of the time, they confirm what you already intuitively know. But they may open a door and give you the impetus you need to change. I feel it's worth the time and money to visit a good vocational counselor or psychologist. He or she can provide you with objective insights.

REFLECT UPON YOUR LIFE

Revelation is seeing something that is hidden from your consciousness. Illumination is to bring something to light with a deeper understanding. Through reflecting on your life, you *reveal* the patterns it contains. Contemplating your life, the way you make mistakes and create successes, is productive. The next step, illumination, is *understanding* what was revealed—what caused those patterns to occur. Age doesn't bring illumination; we know many older people who are not very knowledgeable about themselves.

For example, it is a *revelation* when you realize that you have a high need for people; it is an *illumination* when you understand why. If you have a high need to be liked, it may be because you could not get close, in an emotional sense, to your parents, and thus you want people around you all the time in order to feel wanted.

Remember that personality tends to become more fixated with age. As one physician who had worked with all levels of people in his practice for 50 years told me, "It seems that whatever people are when they're young, they get more of when they're old. If they were warm and caring, they become even more sensitive and deeper toward their fellow man. If they were self-centered and selfish when they were young, they become cantankerous and crabby when they get old!" People who are closed-minded as young adults get downright rigid the older they get. When they are closed to new information, they are unable to make changes and adapt to new circumstances and surroundings.

By reflecting on your life, you challenge your personality to continue to evolve and grow. Overcome the glamour of looking at your life through wishful thinking. Understand your permanent value systems through the impermanent thoughts of the moment. Contemplating your past can be confusing, and you have to learn to rely on yourself to find the occasional clue or thread of self-insight which leads you to illumination. Look at all aspects of yourself—the good and the not-so-good.

We grow by looking back and seeing the consequences of our actions. We learn not to be blindly trusting and gullible. We learn not to allow our emotions to get in the way of decision making. Mature executives learn not to be talked out of their feelings and intuitions. Contemplation allows us to look back on life, to see where we should have had the courage of our convictions. We see where we should have been tougher, where we should have hung in longer when the circumstances got tough.

When we reflect upon our lives, we learn to listen to our own hearts instead of well-meaning but misinformed colleagues. We learn not to place too much faith in other people, but to take responsibility and to have faith in ourselves. We learn that by not taking any risks, we risk everything. Through looking back, we open our minds to wider realizations. Through looking back, we learn the truth of who we are, and we grow in self-knowledge, awareness, and confidence.

Often, looking back at our past, we realize the premises that guided us were false. What we thought was truth really wasn't. For example, we might have thought that becoming involved in a business with a partner made sense. I have found, over the course of my consulting, that most initial business partnerships end in failure. Most business ventures with other people turn out disastrously. When I talk with disgruntled former partners, they tell me that their intuition told them to go it alone. In reality, the reason they wanted a business partner was so they wouldn't have to go it alone. Because of a lack of self-confidence, they didn't believe they were capable of pulling off the enterprise themselves. They sacrificed a great deal to learn that truth about themselves.

Often, executives refuse to take an attractive job transfer. On the outside, they say that they don't want to disrupt their children's lives. But it's really their own fear of change that prevents them from accepting. They create an acceptable illusion so they won't have to confront a weakness.

What you thought was the truth 10 years ago may not be the truth today. The "reality" of 10 years ago is a disappointment now. We wish we could have perceived life more clearly. Bear this simple thought in mind: you and the world have changed a lot over the past 10 years; some of the things you thought were true then have turned out to be false. With a different mindset, history, for you, would be different. Ten years from now, you will have another decade's worth of information. If we had this information today, we would change our minds about a lot of things today, and some of our actions would be different.

When we look over the past 10 years, we see patterns. We attract a certain type of person to us, we behave in a certain way under certain circumstances, we see where we procrastinate. Don't wish that life had been different. Have insight today.

TAKE THE PATH OF GREATEST CHALLENGE

I started my career in a large sales organization. The chairman of the board was a marvelous gentleman of 68 years. He took me under his wing and tried to teach me the ropes of business. Within the first month of my coming on board, he took me to an industry seminar. He wanted me to understand more about our industry and to expose me to some current thinking. I had been trained academically in psychology and counseling, but I was very naive when it came to understanding what marketing and commerce were all about.

He wanted us to go to an early seminar. It started at 7:30 A.M. I arrived at 7:25, and found a seat toward the rear of the auditorium. As I looked down in front of me, whom did I see sitting in the first row with his notebook and pen ready? The chairman, of course.

He was ready to grow, to challenge himself. He wanted new concepts, and wanted to question what he believed in. He later told me he spent an average of three hours per week on self-improvement. He gathers information by challenging his belief system, asking himself *why* he believes something is true. He explained that the vast majority of information presented at most seminars he already knew, but he was always looking for that one little idea he hadn't thought of before, one little scrap of information that would make him a better executive or help his company obtain a higher market share. I have seen several recessions come and go, but his company always gets a little stronger.

I've always admired this chairman for his willingness to take the path of greatest challenge in life. He was born an introvert with a naturally shy attitude toward social interaction. Yet he is personally successful in sales, and built a large sales and marketing organization. Much of his success is due to personal willpower and effort. He took communication skills training courses and was always trying to improve his ability to express ideas and communicate. He is a wonderful example of how people can improve if they are honest with themselves and are willing to expand their minds. He's bright, but I've met many executives I'd consider more intelligent. Yet I know few who understand themselves as well as he does. He truly has a lifelong desire for personal growth. Let's all try to follow his example, and challenge ourselves to grow.

I have conducted many training sessions and have seen many executives in my management seminars. In a short time, I can spot the winners and the losers. The winners have the desire to grow. The losers simply go through the motions because they were told to come. These losers don't know what is said behind their backs. Usually, they are barely hanging on to their jobs and are considered highly expendable. If anyone better comes along, they are generally fired or demoted. They have about as much power within the corporation as the janitor. Upper management wants them to come to my training for "management development," but what they really hope is that they will become more motivated, develop a sense of urgency, and change their attitude to an enthusiastic, optimistic one. Loser managers are generally skeptical about the value of training seminars. Naturally they are skeptical of training—they haven't expanded their knowledge, skills, and abilities in years.

These followers of the path of least challenge seem to have some physical characteristics in common. They are often pudgy, with a slight slump to the shoulder. Their posture is rarely erect or alert; they more often sprawl, legs stretched out in front, slumped down in their seats. They prefer to cast themselves as older, knowledgeable people who, when they speak, comment on "how it is in the real business world." If I call on them directly, they like to attempt to embarrass me by not going along with the role-playing situation. For example, if I'm trying to teach how to establish rapport by asking open-ended questions, they will try to give closed responses, such as a simple "no" to my questions. Then they look around the room with a smirk, thinking they have proven their point: the training doesn't work; they are too smart for it. Usually they bring up the fact that they've tried the particular technique I'm describing, and "it didn't work in real life." When we have role-playing exercises with a partner, they don't attempt to learn the communication skills, but like to "shoot the bull," engaging in general conversation, perhaps trade an old war story or two.

These loser managers are lazy, both physically and mentally. Mental laziness does not mean these losers aren't bright; in fact, many do reasonably well on general intelligence tests. Typically, they get passed over many times for promotions, and end up reporting to someone substantially younger than they are. They feel anger and resentment about this, but they don't say anything to anybody, and to the outside world appear to be "nice guys." They rarely confront the executives above them, and appear to be very supportive and loyal. To those who know them, and especially with vendors, they like to play "hardball." They don't return phone calls or, when they see a vendor, they keep him or her waiting for a few minutes to make sure the vendor understands who is in the power seat. They are slow to establish verbal rapport with vendors, and they try to make the visitor feel as uncomfortable as possible. They play "executive" by exercising power over others, in any form. They are very bitter on the inside. These losers know perfectly well their situation, and their remote chances for further opportunity. Their main goal is to hope the company will continue to do well, and that their position won't be eliminated due to a downturn in the economy.

When I talk with these loser, disgruntled middle-managers, I often find they have some good, valid points on how the company could be improved. I realize, however, that these managers are not the people to be agents of change for the corporate structure. They are only useful in identifying problems. They may have a good understanding of the inconsistencies and seeming stupidities of the policy makers above them, but they have no idea how to get into upper management and improve things one iota. Their main role is to criticize others.

These managers have done exactly the opposite of what our previously mentioned chairman has done. They take the path of least challenge, and the path of least challenge is a path of less good. Loser managers have not challenged themselves or developed their abilities to their highest uses. Their perceptions of life are now fixed and filled with skepticism. Underlying the "nice-guy" exterior is depression. They realize that they're doomed to remain middle-managers. But they have kept themselves there by their refusal to feel uncomfortable. Growth is always initially straining.

When I was a younger consultant, I used to confront these managers, to challenge them to grow and change. I don't bother anymore. They are unwilling to reach crises of self-doubt or pain. Top executives are willing to undergo the pain. Pain is the inevitable result of following the line of greatest challenge in life. You must follow this path in order to overcome your failures and weaknesses. This psychological pain will lead to growth, maturity, and accomplishment. Yes, it's easier not to follow the path of greatest challenge. It's a difficult journey.

The difference in these two approaches to life appears in sharp relief when I analyze potential partners in large accounting and law firms. The most successful members of these organizations realized the value of marketing and sales skills at least 15 years ago. Sales skills are crucial to the continuation and growth of a firm. If you can't sell effectively, you probably won't be invited to be a partner in a top law or accounting firm. Young potential partners, academically bright to the point of being gifted, find themselves voted out because of their lack of sales skills. When this is pointed out to them, they frequently become angry and say, "I didn't go to law school to become a salesman." I have found over the years that sales often is an excellent barometer to find out if people really want to evolve.

People who don't take the time to analyze *why* they don't like to sell have done themselves a disservice. Your ability to sell yourself and your ideas makes a big difference in your career. Many executives feel sales is beneath them, and while it is important, it is not crucial for them to develop sales skills. *How wrong they are.* By being willing to leave their comfort zones, try new techniques, and realize that rejection happens to us all, they could learn to be successful instead of being asked to resign or be passed over.

In my capacity as a management consultant, I have been directly involved in many firings and outplacements. An executive is rarely let go due to a lack of technical expertise. Most commonly, people are let go due to a rigidity of personality that makes it difficult for them to change or adapt to a new mode of thinking. I'll give you an example—one young lawyer particularly comes to mind.

Richard's academic career had been phenomenal. He was his undergraduate class valedictorian and finished second in his class at a prestigious law school. He was hired as an associate by a law firm with which I work.

The senior partners of Richard's firm asked me to give the associates a marketing and sales training class to help them improve their ability to acquire new clients. The first day, I rode up in the elevator with Richard. He didn't acknowledge my greeting and stared straight ahead. Richard sat in the back of the room, and rolled his eyes several times during my talk. Any time there was a role-playing situation, he had to go take a phone call.

During the five years I knew Richard, he took every opportunity let me know just how highly he valued me and my training with comments like, "Still trying to peddle your wares?" and "I know some used-car salesmen who could use your training."

Richard stayed with the firm for seven years, and finally his name came up for partnership. He didn't get a single vote, and he left the firm in disgust. I wasn't surprised—not only did he scoff at the idea of selling his services to clients, he hadn't even bothered to sell himself within the firm.

An old saying in law firms goes something like this: The top students, the "A" people, go on to become professors. The "B" students go on to become judges. The "C" students become members of the firm, and the "D" students become the managing partners! There is a grain of truth in this joke; in the competitive world of law, clients must be courted and developed, and one must be able to do this to hold the top positions. Those "D" students spent some of their time learning how to get along well with people, a powerful skill in "the real world."

Selling skills are important. Even executives with abrasive personalities are kept on board if they understand selling and are willing to go out and do what it takes to bring in business. But for long-term success—to keep the business you bring in—you must genuinely care about the clients and the people you work with.

An Executive with an "Outer" Focus

A case in point is Allen Simmons. Allen was referred to me for outplacement services; he had been fired from his job as vice president of marketing of a large corporation. His severance package included several sessions with me to determine what career pursuit would be positive for him. He had been making approximately $160,000 per year, and had held his job for two years.

Testing showed that Allen was bright—above the 80th percentile in his intellectual ability. Interpersonally, I found him to be a warm, outgoing, sociable person. He was expressive, enthusiastic, and had the ability to be politely assertive, all the qualities of a natural salesperson. What had happened? Why hadn't Allen made it as vice president of marketing?

Further testing revealed a more complicated personality than my interview suggested. He tended to be content with his natural abilities, and didn't push himself. Under stress, he could be argumentative and closed-minded. From these small, common personality faults, an important clue emerged: he did not engender the esteem of his peers.

Allen was a tightwad. As a general rule, tightwads don't do well in upper-level management. When you are slow to pick up a check, people observe this and remember it. He never picked up the check when eating with his staff, a real mistake for a boss. All businesspeople keep a general accounting ledger in their minds. When you don't pick up checks at least half the time, it reveals a part of your personality that people distrust. His staff resented the fact that Allen never wanted to pay for anything—except with the company's money.

Allen also had a problem with following through on his commitments. When it came to sticking with a project over a long haul, he tended to come up short. When there wasn't any "flash" to the situation or project, he lost interest. Any large assignment in a corporation requires willpower and trudging. The ability to trudge is a useful trait to acquire. Allen thought he was above it. He didn't have the willpower to keep striving toward a goal unless there was lots of recognition along the way.

Allen is a perfect example of someone who shouldn't have moved from sales to management. He has a great deal of pride in how he is perceived, so an upper-level management position seemed a natural for him. But on a deeper level, he didn't want to manage others—he wanted their admiration. He had little desire to direct others' activities. He wanted to be popular, to be included on party invitation lists and happenings around town. He had a problem with pride; he didn't believe he could be wrong about a situation. On more than one occasion, the president of the firm pointed out to him that he had made a customer angry. Allen never really believed this. He shrugged it off, saying, "That customer is always mad about something anyway," or, "That customer is so stupid, he didn't even know what he wanted." This smug self-confidence, combined with his cheapness and his desire to argue instead of resolving conflicts diplomatically, cost him in the long run.

Allen won't have problems getting another job. With his good looks, friendly handshake, strong eye contact, and impeccable grooming, he can fool most personnel officers. Be on the lookout for this type. They're hard to spot until they've been on board for a year, but watch for these signs of an "Allen" in your midst. You'll gradually realize that situations don't get resolved the way they're supposed to. Sales don't pick up as much as they should, and there is a lack of follow-through. People, first enamored, begin to lose respect and interest. When you weed out the culprit, your situation will dramatically improve.

Allen didn't know himself well at all. He was concerned with the outer man—the one society sees. He overlooked the inner man—the one the mirror sees. In the long run, your subordinates and other team members recognize the real you. The only person you can fool for very long is yourself. See what others see about you, and change what you don't like. It's the only way to change the way you're perceived.

THE UNCONSCIOUS DEFENSE MECHANISMS

Defense mechanism is the term mental health professionals use to describe the unconscious process that prevents people from understanding their true reasons for behaving the way they do. Defense mechanisms keep you from getting to know yourself. *Unconscious* means that you are not aware of or don't know what causes you to behave in a certain way. Defense mechanisms can be viewed as a way of escaping reality. There are many reasons people do not look at themselves realistically. Psychiatry has identified a number of common defense mechanisms. These defense mechanisms operate in business, too. They prevent executives from being aware of who they really are.

Compensation

Compensation is an unconscious defense mechanism in which people attempt to hide real or imagined deficiencies by portraying themselves differently than they really are. For example, executives who are aggressive to the point of being obnoxious may have deep inferiority complexes, but want to appear tough and authoritarian to others because of a fear of exposure. I once consulted with a company which was having trouble with an executive of this type. He was relatively short in stature, with a pear-shaped build. You simply could not have a decent conversation with this individual; he was always smirking and criticizing his surroundings, his environment, and other people. He made snide, cutting remarks to everyone he met. He wanted to be viewed as a dynamic, powerful man. On a deeper level, he was fearful and didn't know himself well, so he compensated.

Denial and Repression

Denial is a defense mechanism often used to resolve and allay anxiety by pretending that something simply isn't true. Executives often believe they are popular and have the support of their people because of their "leadership qualities." But sometimes the people under them think that they are fools, and have little, if any, respect for them. On a conscious level, this realization would be intolerable to the executive, so he denies it. He tells himself he is a super guy who has loyalty, respect, and love from "his people."

We all spend some time in denial. As a consultant, I help executives and companies examine themselves and overcome their denial of truth. Companies are using denial when they refuse to recognize the superiority of a competitor's methodology or product, or when they refuse to acknowledge internal problems. One company I worked with went to great lengths to show me that the executive team functioned as a solid unit and got along well. In reality, it was well known throughout the company that members of the top management team had little in common and no respect for each other. The resulting splits greatly affected the company's bottom line and potential, but the team denied there were any problems.

Sometimes company presidents refuse to allow climate or attitude surveys to be administered, or if they do, they take out any questions that pertain to how they are viewed as leaders—they would just as soon not know. Executives can also not openly and candidly ask their clients and customers what they don't like about their product or service. Thus they don't receive truthful feedback to correct and upgrade the service. Good, solid companies quickly get into trouble when defense mechanisms result in an "ivory tower" approach to business. The decision makers deny or repress any unfavorable information, and instead focus on "strategy." They are surprised when sales figures turn out to be a far cry from their statistical projections.

One of denial's biggest allies is *repression*—keeping unpleasant information in the subconscious mind, away from conscious awareness. Repression is often a subtle process. Chief executive officers do not like to hear negative feedback about their company's performance and prospects. The managers shape the behavior of their managers by punishing them—overtly or covertly—when they provide negative feedback. The managers begin to withhold negative information as a result. One by one, over a period of time, the superior executives leave the company. Weaker people, happy to get good-paying jobs, fill the vacancies. They quickly recognize the game being played and readily take part in repressing information too. The company's collective perception of reality, heavily influenced by safety needs, begins to warp. The company continues to lose market share, and eventually the corporate equivalent of a breakdown occurs. The company's "reality" is completely different from the truth as the result of denial and repression.

Idealization

Idealization is a defense mechanism which can operate consciously (known to yourself) or unconsciously. Idealization is the process of overestimating an admired aspect or attribute of another. We see idealization in "mentoring" when a young executive is assigned to or taken under the wing of an older executive. Young executives frequently overestimate a mentor's ability level and place too much faith in his or her judgment. This situation usually resolves itself badly when the younger executive realizes that the emperor has no clothes—the older executive has traits that greatly handicap him or her. As a general rule, the older you get, the less you idealize other people. It is certainly acceptable to admire the fine qualities of others, but at the same time you must realize that there is virtually nobody who has "got it all together." We're all a little flawed. Accept the positives and negatives of people with a practical indifference; that is, admire their fine qualities and accept their negative traits. Don't idealize anyone in your life. This sets *you* up for disappointment and retards *your* emotional growth.

Identification

Often, idealization leads to *identification* with another; you unconsciously pattern yourself after a person you idealize. Identification plays a major role in the development of personality, especially when we're young. When you talk like someone else, or attempt to use the same pattern of words as someone you admire, you are identifying with them.

Ultimately, this leads to the deterioration of your maturity. Again, admire certain traits of others, but don't overly identify with those traits and consider them your own. This blocks your inner awareness of your own talents and abilities.

Projection

Another defense mechanism which prevents understanding of self is *projection*. What you don't like or find unacceptable in yourself is attributed to or projected on others. An authoritarian/dictator type may consider himself to be a dynamic leader. He considers other executives little Napoleons! He thinks other executives at his same level are jerks, and is confused as to why they don't recognize or understand his superior talents. A manager who lacks self-confidence and cannot make decisions because he or she is afraid to be wrong may project that all the executives above them are poor decision makers, that they "just don't make things happen" the way the manager could. These people refuse to acknowledge that *they* are the ones who are clogging the system with *their* inefficiencies: a lack of conviction or a need to control.

Rationalization

Rationalization is an unconscious defense mechanism in which individuals attempt to justify or make tolerable to themselves behavior or feelings that otherwise would be judged intolerable. We see this when people take advantage of others in business deals, and say, "The other person would have taken advantage of me first, if only given the opportunity." People rationalize their own unethical business dealings to themselves. I also see rationalization in executives who say "The reason I can't get ahead is because my boss doesn't really like me." Presidents generally promote those people who are the most highly qualified. Being passed over generally means the company feels you are not qualified. We all hear rationalizations when work that is promised to us at a certain time isn't ready. We're given every justification in the world, except the real reason—they weren't committed enough!

Substitution

Substitution is a defense mechanism in which an unattainable goal is replaced by one which is more attainable or acceptable. People who can't make it to upper-level management may try to obtain positions in civic or church organizations that provide them with leadership and visibility, or they may become highly involved in their family. By being socially acceptable, they make up for not having achieved their business goals. No one is suggesting you should not spend quality time with your family; this is one of the cornerstones of a happy and balanced existence. However, substitution is common among mid-level managers when they do not find occupational success at the level they had once hoped. The substituted goal is rarely as rewarding as the original goal.

Regression

Regression is a partial return to earlier patterns of reacting or thinking. It is another form of defense that executives use when confronted with a situation in which they are over their head conceptually. Successful financial people are often detail- and number-oriented, not people-oriented. When given a top-level management position, they sometimes can't handle the responsibility of motivating and counseling their people. This problem becomes particularly acute when sales are down and a marketing drive is needed. In their role as president, they could be very helpful in sales but spend a great deal of time in "going over the numbers." They become almost fanatical about examining expense reports, rechecking and quantifying everything with which they come into contact. They are essentially regressing back to an earlier form of behavior that they know well. This regression provides them with relief from the anxiety of having to become more actively involved in the marketing arena.

In order to progress in your career, your old ways of behaving must give way to new ways and new modes of thinking. The old must constantly be reevaluated and refurbished. At the beginning of the fall season, many people reevaluate their wardrobe. They reassess their needs and compare those needs to the clothes on hand. A classic Hart Shaffner Marx suit in good condition remains in the closet. A double-knit leisure suit from 20 years ago must go. A pinpoint cotton dress shirt, always a favorite, is now worn out and must be replaced.

In this same manner, take stock of your behaviors. Review how you deal with subordinates. Are you fair and honest? Do you have regard for their ideas and feelings? If so, keep that behavior. But if you basically manage people the same way you managed them when leisure suits were in style, your management style is just as antiquated. Review how you deal with vendors. Do you insist on expensive lunches and gifts before you do business? If so, throw that behavior out with the leisure suit. Review how you treat clients. Are you honest but perhaps not forthcoming? Update this behavior. Be honest and open with clients. Consider this your new pinpoint cotton shirt! Avoid concentrating your energies on the part of your job that appeals to you personally. In unfamiliar settings, we all revert to what we think we understand best. As an upper-level executive, you must be well rounded and able to concentrate on those things that you do not wish to do.

As an executive, your job is to make decisions which allow your company to grow and prosper. To make a good decision, you gather all the information you can, evaluate the options, and then act. Gather all the information you can about *yourself* through introspection so you can make enlightened decisions about *your* direction.

POWER INSIGHT TIPS

1. You are solely responsible for acquiring information about yourself.
2. The more you understand about yourself, the more you can control your thoughts and behavior.
3. Don't let your ego get in the way of your self-knowledge.
4. Analyze why you like certain people and dislike others. What can you learn about yourself by your predilections and associations?
5. Don't be intimidated by personality tests—they are a useful tool for growth.
6. Reflect upon your life to find deeper meaning.
7. Challenge yourself by overcoming your weaknesses and taking the path of greatest challenges.
8. Challenge yourself to assess what defense mechanisms are preventing your executive growth.

Chapter 2

Power Growth

Maturity can be defined as the acceptance of your role in life which gives you an inner sense of security. Think of it as a state of consciousness that uses more of the nobler elements: wisdom, compassion, courage, and competence. Knowledge lays the framework for maturity, and wisdom is the outgrowth of knowledge. Buddhism teaches that Nirvana (freedom from delusion and psychic tension) is obtained through being kind, being resolute in the seeking of truth, being able to hold your tongue under stress, taking the right decisive action, being self-disciplined, giving your full effort, and controlling your emotions. Mature executives manifest these psychological characteristics. Maturity can thus be viewed as a global human condition which encompasses all faiths and races. As the world is developing a global economy, so too are we developing a global consciousness.

There are traces of maturity in all of us. In order to gain maturity, you must have self-knowledge, as discussed in the first chapter. Expanding self-awareness also expands your consciousness. *Consciousness* has been defined in many ways: the aggregate of your inner feelings, your perceptions, the reactions of your intellect to the environment, the interpretation of your thoughts and feelings to yourself, the outermost tip of awareness used by the personality to focus on ideas, events, and facts from moment to moment.

Top executives have an inner urge to expand their consciousness. This is practical, worthwhile, and necessary in order to achieve at a higher level. When you have a higher-level consciousness, you have the power of self-knowledge. This is the most significant key to success.

With a higher-level consciousness, you begin to realize the truly important relationship is the one between you and your definition of God. Other aspects of your life are important, but they are subordinate to this one critical relationship. Your fundamental definition and deep belief of this is the key to your value system and the key to all decision making.

We see many people with status and power who lack a higher degree of consciousness and maturity. They give in to their lower-level impulses. We have all met people who have accumulated a great deal of money, but for whom we have little respect. When we get to know them, we realize they aren't particularly happy with life. Often, they're concerned with impressing others so they can be impressed with themselves. The evolved executive defines success monetarily, but also defines a successful life as spiritual growth that leads to maturity.

Intelligence is an ingredient for higher consciousness, but like people with money, we've all met intelligent people who occupy a low-level position in their company. Because of immaturity, they cannot take the burden of leadership. They are handicapped by their personality or their poor ability to handle stress, which is, ultimately, a lack of faith.

Most psychologists agree that intelligence is a fairly constant quality throughout life; intelligence is not really subject to change. On intelligence tests, most of us fall within the average levels, with an I.Q. between 90 and 110. Contrary to what many parents want to believe, their children also fall into these average ranges.

If we have roughly average intelligence, how do we get to upper-level management? Unless you can dazzle your way to the top with your intellectual prowess, your only avenue is to grow in a psychological sense, through self-knowledge, to reach maturity. Maturity is an area you *can* increase. The ability to develop maturity is as good as—or perhaps even better than—being born extremely bright.

Think of constant desire as selfishness governed by greed. Constant desire hides higher-order truth. The more desire(s) you have, the more you are governed by negative emotions, which distort reality and cause unhappiness. Some immature executive behaviors are:

- Blaming others for our mistakes.
- An egotistic need to take credit for new ideas.
- Subtly setting up intra-company rivalries.
- Jealousy, anger, and revenge seeking.
- Pouting.
- The desire to dominate simply to feed the ego.
- The inability to handle negative feedback or criticism.
- The need to appear intelligent to others.

A TEACHER TURNED EXECUTIVE

Ed Marshall was 46 years old at the time I profiled him. He was being considered for a regional vice presidential position that paid approximately $175,000 per year. Ed had an interesting background that did not lend itself to high-level corporate work, yet my client company was interested in hearing what I thought. Ed had been a school administrator for 20 years. He had a master's degree in English. Ordinarily, this is not the type of person who does well in a competitive business organization. They often lack the necessary background skills. Also, there is a widespread belief that the educational system is slow, somewhat stodgy, and not given to developing high-level achievers. People who come from a noncompetitive administrative position in the public sector often have difficulty in a market-driven, tension-filled, aggressive business.

Nonetheless, Ed had retired from teaching after 20 years, and had taken a job as a first-line supervisor. In two years, he had moved up two levels. I interviewed and evaluated Ed, and I recommended him for the position. At this point, he is considered the best vice president in the company, doing a very solid job.

When the company divides the country into two major regions, he will be named as senior vice president in charge of operations for one-half of the United States. He is going to have a very prosperous, full business career, and has earned the esteem and regard of his company and industry.

Testing showed that Ed's intelligence is in the upper ranges of average. His most pronounced trait is his emotional maturity. This is what impressed me. He has an open mind, and is willing to grow through being receptive to new information. He is very intuitive, yet objective. In addition to his master's in English, he has a degree and teaching certificate in math. His advanced degrees, with roughly average intelligence, are testimonial to his ability to be self-disciplined. This is a key characteristic trait of the emotionally mature. This helped him develop his analytical, quantitative approach to the world. His blend of quantitative abilities and verbal, intuitive skills is what set him apart.

Ed is also very honest. In the beginning, perhaps, he was naive. He had a more liberal outlook on the world than many business executives do. Like many educators, he has an underlying need for affection and appreciation from people. Occasionally, his decision making reflects this need for affection. In his first two years, he toughened up but kept his honesty. He has an ideal way of viewing the world and his role in it. He has strong religious beliefs, but certainly does not preach. He has a highly ethical, moral value system, and can adapt to change and deal with irate, obnoxious people with grace and aplomb. He sets his goals high, and his willpower and drive are excellent. His decision-making style is to accumulate carefully all the facts about a situation, form his opinion, and then act.

Ed is also a loyal person. You can count on him. He has beautifully smooth interpersonal social skills, and can make a person feel immediately relaxed. He is not strongly extroverted, but engages in conversation easily. He has the ability to handle criticism. He gives compliments liberally. He enjoys social recognition, but his ego is very much under control. He enjoys managing others, but can certainly take direction from upper management.

He has a very strong ability to withstand stress. Ed is patient, understands people, and is forgiving. I have never seen him flustered, even in a very stressful situation. I admire Ed, and feel that his career will reach ever-growing heights.

AN INTROSPECTIVE EXECUTIVE

Another executive who I believe has been successful because of his emotional maturity is Norman Evans. At the time Norman asked me to profile him, he had just been named president of his company. He was 35 years old, and worked his way up through the firm quickly. Norman is well-liked and respected by those who know him. He wanted me to profile him to help him with his management skills, because he realized that this was a big jump for him, and he wanted my opinion on where he needed to improve.

Testing showed that Norman is a friendly, outgoing person, kindly and socially participating. He is venturesome, and likes to interact with people. His value system tends to be very conservative. He related to me that he was brought up in a rule-oriented environment with a strong religious base. He is not close-minded, however, like so many highly conservative people, and is willing to grow and learn. He also is intuitive, and very empathetic in appraising situations.

On his profile, he listed his positive qualities as his ability to get along with people, good judgment, dependable, competent, well-rounded, with a dedicated faith. He listed his negative qualities as not being aggressive enough, impatient at times, lacking self-confidence, and having difficulty saying no. Norman's accurate depiction of himself is the key to his strength. A mature person can honestly admit he or she doesn't have enough self-confidence, or that he or she isn't aggressive enough. I agree that Norman has problems in being assertive. He doesn't like to tell people bad news; he wants to be accommodating, and is easily sold on a situation. He is also very sensitive to criticism, and as a result, even though he knows he shouldn't be, he is very accepting of flattery. A person's sensitivity to criticism usually equals his or her vulnerability to flattery. Flattery wins Norman over because he has the need for social approval.

Norman sets his goals high, and is honest and open in his approach to others. In order to be successful, he will have to develop his team-building skills. Right now, he is overly self-sufficient and doesn't delegate or "group-think" enough.

I also feel that Norman needs more nurturing in his life from his spouse, who tends to be cold, non-expressive, and noncomplimentary. If he got more of this psychological need filled at home, he would not look for it on the job. I also feel he didn't completely connect with his parents, didn't receive much praise from them, and that also underlies his need for acceptance by others.

I do believe Norman will be successful in his presidency. I plan to work with him and help him as best I can. I feel his intelligence, intuition, his genuine sensitivity and caring for people, and his overall maturity will be the ingredients for his success.

SURVIVAL INSTINCTS

The terms *maturity* and *mental health* are interchangeable. Both concepts germinate from the same seed: controlling your lower-order energies, your desires or survival instincts. The more you control these, the more joy you find in life and your career.

Executives commonly exhibit a high need for dominance through personality testing. The need to dominate is a manifestation of the survival instinct. Executives are often driven to be executives because of survival instincts manifested through dominant behavior. Dominant people have a need to control their environments, including the people around them. Research shows that executives with a high dominance need tend to rise in corporations, provided relatively high intelligence is also present. The evolved, mature executive must strive to understand this drive, to go from being control-oriented to being goal-focused.

The mature executive's attitude and temperament lend themselves more to *serving* fellow executives and employees rather than dominating them. Competitive attitudes, especially within a company, are rapidly giving way to cooperative attitudes.

Evolved executives realize that the big picture is more important than individual control. As one executive told me, "The world is moving rapidly. Knowledge is expanding at an exponential rate. We need the expertise and talents of our entire management team if we're going to compete in this market." He has created a management structure that fosters creative ideas from each team member in a noncritical environment. The only rule in his brainstorming session is, "No judgment." After they've gotten ideas flowing, they work out details and the best solution.

An Example of Lower-Order Drives

Wayne Rogers had reached the level of vice president of marketing and sales for his corporation. The marketing department, four district sales managers and a total of 175 salespeople, all reported to him. His income level was approximately $225,000 a year.

I didn't test Wayne for his position; however, I was surprised to find him calling me because he had been fired from his company because of sexual harassment.

Wayne had an excellent career going. But a careful look at his resume showed that he had jumped around quite a bit. He managed to have good references, and employers tended to overlook his job jumping because of his good looks and pleasant, intelligent way of expressing himself.

To those around him, however, particularly at his peer level, he seemed aggressive, brusque, and demanding. His tendency was to overcome his fellow executives rather than gain their consensus. When I discussed his situation with several of his peers, they laughed and exhibited a great deal of delight over his dismissal.

It turns out Wayne was sexually harassing six different women at various locations around the country, all of whom told the president that they would go to court unless he was fired. When we looked further into his past, we learned that he was fired by several of his other employers for the same reason.

I profiled him for some outplacement services. Unquestionably, he was intelligent. He was bright, creative, and could think abstractly. Unlike most marketing types, he had a good mind for detail. He set his goals high, and had the persistence to meet those goals. He had a huge ego. He signed his name in large, flowing letters that took up a great deal of space.

Profile results showed that he was bossy, intimidating, and could even be brutal. He liked to take executives on at meetings, pointing out flaws in their thinking, and reminding them of what they'd said previously. Because of this, creativity and brainstorming were virtually nonexistent at this company. This was one of the reasons that the company's profits were flat and growth projections failed. Several executives had vowed to get even behind his back.

In a one-on-one setting, particularly if you didn't know Wayne, he appeared enthusiastic and expressive, and could sell himself very effectively. He was particularly good at a cocktail party, where he was charming, cheerful, and socially venturesome. However, he tended to dominate the conversations of those he considered inferior. Underneath his sociable exterior was a suspicious, skeptical, and distrusting individual. On a deeper level, he was insecure. He used a lot of bluff and puff, but underneath was a great deal of guilt and tension. This was a true case of compensation.

Wayne is an excellent example of the inability to discipline the lower-order desires, particularly his sexual energy. The only way he could relate to others was by dominating them. Having an open, trusting, true relationship was virtually impossible. I met his wife once. She was rather mouse-like, yielding to his every demand. She was more like his servant.

Wayne described his strong qualities as his intelligence, decisiveness, logic, and work ethic. He described his bad points as impatience and a short temper. I agree with him, and also felt that he was a sneaky, secretive person, one who never engendered trust. People who can't engender trust in those under them can't expect loyalty.

The straw that broke the camel's back was obviously his desire for sexual experiences in order to dominate women. Despite his strength, because of his demanding nature and his inability to get others to trust him, I think he's doomed for failure in the long run. I feel that if he could have the self-discipline and control to keep his sexuality on an even keel, find some spirituality, and look at himself honestly, it would make a difference in his life.

THE HARD-CHARGERS

Dominant traits can help one get ahead in the executive world. Being tough-minded and aggressive, a young "hard-charger" can climb the corporate ladder, leaving a few bodies along the way. A hard-charger justifies these tactics with a survival of the fittest theory of business. Some of these young, aggressive executives believe it's necessary to "kick butt," and further believe this ability to do the tougher assignments separates them from weaker coworkers.

These traits may *initially* help an executive climb the corporate ladder. Through promotion and recognition, his or her perception of what it takes to be a top executive is selectively reinforced. In other words, he or she believes that the theory of survival of the fittest is the important attitude for an executive to have. This executive is still playing "king of the hill" from childhood days.

Over a period of time, such an executive begins to feel superior to others based on his or her achievement record. Employees whom they leapfrogged over and treat shabbily may be intimidated, they hold an inner grudge, and will get even if the opportunity presents itself.

After 15 or 20 years, our young hard-chargers are now 40. They have done well and come up through the ranks successfully. Unfortunately, they do not realize that weak people are easily dominated. Additionally, competent employees, because of life circumstances, may be in a lower position than their ability warrants. I have often seen managers who are much more competent than the bosses above them, but because of some set of life events and circumstances, they aren't where they should be. Hard-charging, aggressive executives, feeling superior and blinded by their own ambition, aren't really aware of the animosity they created. They feel they are genetically superior to others, and deserve to be in command.

At the vice presidential level, and most certainly at the senior vice presidential level, an executive needs the support and team efforts of his or her peers. At this level, the others in the management team are usually not easily intimidated or bullied. Higher-order facilitating and consensus-building executive styles are now needed. The dominating executive begins to realize the other members of the executive team are forming a union against him or her. He or she is confused as to how to go about establishing dominance over this peer group. The hard-charger didn't learn the art of making friends along the career path. The hard-charger has chosen to set himself or herself up for failure by these dominating tendencies. The other team members will eventually gang up on a young hard-charger and say negative things about him or her to the president. Team members begin to shape the president's mind that the hard-charger is not a good team player, not wanted on the team.

Dominance must be balanced with maturity before it is truly a facilitator in an upper-level executive's career. Aspire to an executive position, don't desire it. Aspiration and emotional maturity is what makes a top executive.

A highly dominant executive, whom I profiled using personality tests, met with me to discuss the results. As people who wish to establish dominance over vendors will do, he kept me waiting outside his office "until he was ready to see me." As I entered his office, he remained behind his desk in order to reach over to shake hands. After a quick rapport, he went into a lengthy explanation of motivational theory which he knew I was familiar with—I'm a former psychologist. The real reason behind his discourse was his need to dominate and demonstrate his intelligence. I believe he also wanted to postpone going over the test results to reduce the time we had to spend on them, and just go over the highlights, nothing in-depth or threatening. This was a form of a defense mechanism.

After 15 or 20 minutes of this rambling, I began to understand what the other executives on the team had been telling me. This guy was a pain, always mouthing off, and immaturely aggressive. He was not able to balance dominance with maturity.

LEAVING OUR PAST

We must leave our past in order to grow. When you master something you originally found challenging, your feeling of control leads to your belief in your innate power. People who stay in their mental comfort zones unchallenged have no opportunity to develop this belief.

I have seen this demonstrated in new salespeople who can't cold-call effectively. Generally, salespeople who are reluctant to cold-call take themselves too seriously, are overly sensitive, or are suspicious of others. When you take yourself too seriously, you have an inability to laugh at life and yourself. Be enthusiastic, and be able to poke fun at yourself. It's fun to try and cold-call when you don't take yourself too seriously; if you distance yourself from your own ego, the process becomes more enjoyable, less like drudgery. When you're overly sensitive, and wear your feelings on your sleeve, cold-calling is psychologically threatening.

You may be asking why executives would ever have to cold-call. In fact, they usually don't. In order to be really successful, however, they must be *capable* of doing it. Reluctance to do so, or to even consider the idea, is an indicator of the executive that is limited.

When executives tell me privately that they could never cold-call, I've noticed they often won't take social risks, are not spontaneous, and are highly controlled. They don't like to talk about themselves in any meaningful way or get close to others physically or psychologically. There is also a degree of subtle cynicism. They are mortified by the fear of being humiliated. They like to be considered smart and professional by others. They have a hard time showing excitement. I've noticed in my seminars that people who say they hate to cold-call also hate role-playing. They are obsessed with their images. They are the ones who hate taking psychological or self-improvement tests.

Public speaking is another threatening business challenge which is important to your career. You may initially feel uncomfortable in this role. By practicing and learning to put yourself in an uncomfortable situation, your horizons grow. It's uncomfortable to face your deficiencies, but if you do, they can't limit you.

YOU BE THE JUDGE

Many situations are difficult judgment calls between selfishness and ordinary, bottom-line business success. To illustrate this gray area, let's look at a well-known scenario of the entrepreneur buyout, in which a smart, capable person got an idea, built a sizable business, then decided to sell out and walk away rich. The point of view changes depending on who's telling the story.

Other executives I've worked with don't like to discipline or provide directives to their employees. Yet, without structure, feedback, and correction, the infrastructure of a business doesn't work in harmony. Once these executives realize they have a high desire to be liked that impedes their ability to effectively make decisions, they can overcome it. They begin to understand that managing others requires self-confidence, the ability to motivate through listening, and occasionally, decisive intervention. Their need to be liked should not be a force that greatly influences them. The need to be liked must be overcome in order to be a true professional.

An entrepreneurial client of mine was a smart businessman. He got a good idea, and had the tenacity and fortitude to build a sizable business. After a number of years, he found a substantial buyer to buy him out. This is a 50-year-old man who cashed out for $40 million.

Besides the entrepreneur, there were five people who hung with him through thick and thin, and helped him build the business. They weren't as smart as he was, nor were they taking the risks, but they certainly made a solid, substantial contribution. When the decisions were really examined, it was clear that the entrepreneur called the shots. The management team was composed of operators and implementers.

The entrepreneur, a secretive individual, handled the negotiations for the sale of the company through the chief financial officer, who was sworn to secrecy. After the lawyers crossed all the t's and dotted all the i's, a deal was finally cut. There was a big wad of money on the table for the entrepreneur. The ethical question was, how much did the entrepreneur plan to give his loyal management team? He had no legal obligation to give anything. It came down to his value system.

In many situations like this, I've seen the entrepreneur grab most of the bucks and distance himself from his former team—both psychologically and physically. That was certainly the case in this example. The team was dismayed and angry. They didn't receive a nickel of the $40 million.

Whose fault was it? Could the blame go to either party? The managers on the team knew long before this that the entrepreneur called most or all of the shots. He kept the books pretty well hidden over the years. The bonuses he gave were never generous, only enough to keep people on board. Does the management team have any right to gripe? They should have known that leopards don't change their spots. If they look at the situation objectively, they'll realize that they made choices over the past years, and stayed because of fear of change, or a lack of self-confidence. They didn't want to take the risk to leave; they took the path of least challenge.

On the other hand, one could say that the owner was selfish. He could have helped out his loyal managers who faithfully carried out his orders for so many years. They put up with his emotional, selfish, and egocentric management style. They were deferential, supportive, and covered up for his weaknesses. Couldn't he have been more generous?

Most selfish entrepreneurs who sell out will rationalize their greed. They figure they don't really owe their people very much. After all, they made the business happen. They gave their employees a good paycheck, helped their kids get through college. What more could the employees want, or expect?

How would you describe this judgment call? Would it be "That's the way the cookie crumbles," or "That jerk could have been more generous"?

On a deeper level, I think these entrepreneurs realize that they've given in to the lower-order desire of selfishness. Like all human beings, they feel an obligation to humanity. Although they have repressed it, it still affects them. I've seen entrepreneurs who have swindled people out of millions give a great deal of money to a church or a charity, trying to convince themselves that they aren't a reincarnated Scrooge—to dispel the guilty aftermath of greed. People who got rich this way may suddenly go into a deep depression "for no apparent reason." They get a lot of mileage out of the appreciative church congregations, however.

The one thing the entrepreneur from the sell-out scenario is missing is genuine love and appreciation from the team. It would have been very rewarding to look back with his team on how well they had done together. Because of his lower-order desire, love can't be obtained. The entrepreneur is trapped within his own prison—the prison of selfishness. He could have been so much happier in life if he had spread a little prosperity through generosity. He would have kept the love and support of his infrastructure. When we are young and when we are old we depend upon the kindness of others for our survival and happiness. Later in life, we may want the help of those people again. The entrepreneur's only ROI (return on investment) when he is old and feeble will be resentment and bitterness from his once-loyal team.

You must decide for yourself what value system to utilize in your business career. Remember this basic principle of energy which is an old metaphysical proverb: "Any negative energy that you send out will bring that same energy three times back to you." Any act of unselfishness or kindness brings back the same form and degree of energy. On some level of awareness, we all realize the basic truth, "As you sow, so shall you reap," or "What goes around, comes around." We know that if we act unethically or selfishly, this will come back to haunt us in the long run. Unethical businesspeople can make fortunes, but they never seem to find joy.

I once knew a very successful business owner who built a large chain of outlets. He was divorced, and his only daughter refused even to talk to him. He ate Thanksgiving and Christmas dinner alone. The root of his loneliness was that he took advantage of people constantly. He could never have a true friend because he thought all people were to be used to fill his agenda in life. In a negotiation, just when he was about to sign, he would ask for one more thing. This is a familiar ruse; get the other party psychologically and emotionally committed to the deal so they will give up something just to get the deal done. This guy took the principle to the extreme.

He has fallen on hard times now due to the major real estate devaluation of the early 1990s. Everyone I talk to is delighted that this fellow is finally getting his due. Bankers he used to take advantage of are now really enjoying foreclosing on his properties every chance they get. He had lots of lunch dates when he was worth $200 million; now he lunches alone.

Businesspeople must decide for themselves what the line between selfishness and their ethical systems are. In business, we tend to expect people to be more selfish than Mother Teresa, but hopefully they are more generous than Scrooge. There is a difference psychologically between making a good profit and living a good life, and being a gluttonous, materialistic monster.

Our selfishness is an offshoot of the survival instinct, the fear of death. Therefore, the feeling is natural. But we also have an underlying need to be kind to enjoy life. We have a need to rise in maturity and be detached from our lower-order instincts. There is an answer for each of us, but it is always an individual one. Executives must decide for themselves and live with their decisions.

DEVELOPING A SENSE OF PROPORTION

As an executive, develop the right sense of proportion regarding your contribution to the success of the company. Have some humility. Be sure credit and recognition are given to others.

Graphologists—handwriting analysts—say your signature is a representation of how you want the world to see you. Your signature makes a statement about your social self-presentation. Is your signature big or fancy? The bigger your signature, the more attention you crave.

A president I know, through inheritance from a wealthy family, managed to get hold of a number of franchises. When he took over the company, the franchises were valuable, but not unbelievably so. A successful marketing campaign by the parent company dramatically increased the franchises' worth. Everyone who held one did extremely well, regardless of their management skill. This president thinks his franchises have done well because of his incredible ability. He feels he is a genius.

Even though he is doing extremely well financially, he still hasn't found any measure of inner peace. He has been divorced three times. He drinks heavily. His signature is four times as big as his regular writing. If he could accept the fact that he's been lucky, be grateful for that luck, and learn to increase his skill level, not only would he be happier, he would have humility. It's interesting how the two go hand in hand.

DEALING WITH BUSINESS CRISES

The emotionally mature executive realizes that business crises are part of the job. Business crises are points of examination of their personal strengths. When crises are surmounted, crisis-produced vision and confidence become the building blocks of maturity. Crises foster compassion and understanding, for they draw on the resources of the heart. Crises transform knowledge into wisdom.

All businesses go through different types of crises. For example, companies are getting "downsized" every day. Good, honest, loyal, hardworking people get laid off. People, like businesses, are having to become more entrepreneurial and create diverse ways to make a living. People who were laid off often come to believe that it was the best thing to have happened to them. Some exceed their previous lifestyle monetarily by opening up their own businesses. Others, when laid off, panic and take the first job offered them, and their lifestyles plummet as a result.

Living in Texas in the 1980s and 1990s, I've seen lots of people go through bankruptcy. They've either gained in emotional maturity by accepting that it was part of life, or they've aged 20 years in just two, become withdrawn, and lost their self-confidence. Nobody who runs a business or who is an upper-level executive wants to go bankrupt or get fired. But be prepared psychologically for difficult times. Strive to make each day happy, and don't allow yourself the selfishness of depression. The optimist in business is more valuable than the pessimist.

I've seen many businesses lose their best customer. When I left my former company, I agreed to be a consultant to them. I was a loyal, dedicated executive for them for five years, and a dedicated consultant to them for two more. One day, the president called me and said he wanted to make a change in business strategy; my services would no longer be needed.

The loss of his business was particularly hard on me. Not only had I given seven years of my life to it, I had been extremely loyal and gone beyond the call of duty to help them. I resented the president's decision. All sorts of things went through my mind: vowing to get even, going straight to his main competitor and offering my services.

Now that I've been in business for some time, I realize that all businesses eventually lose the customer that put them in business to begin with. At first, the loss of the significant customer causes blame, discouragement, and fear. But after the shock subsides, you begin to realize that reliance on that customer covered up weaknesses in your services and systems. The customer was partially an illusion. You believed your business had more stability and strength than it actually had. By losing a customer, this illusion is shattered, causing a greater awareness of the truth of the situation. Truth, when faced directly, causes strength. Change brings pain—the shattering of the old form of reality to make a new form of reality. People don't fear change, they fear the destruction of the old form.

When crisis occurs, you must keep your mind on your original goal, your original intent. That is the source of your strength. There are going to be disappointments and losses along the way. The goal must be the magnetic energy that pulls you through the crisis. Constantly have your business direct its energy toward the focus of the business.

Looking back on the loss of my most important original customer, I realize I could have done some things differently to keep him as a customer. I could have paid closer attention to his account and been more creative in my consulting. Losing that client was terrific for my business. I realized that by keeping him and keeping the company I was relying on a poorer quality of business than I could have had if I'd gone out, hustled, and developed better clientele. Also, it's hard to be a hero when you worked for a company and now consult to that company . . . they know your psychological warts too well!

I'm not suggesting you shouldn't care if you lose a good customer. I *am* saying that customers' needs, values, and directions change, and we are going to lose 10 to 20 percent of our customers every year. We just have to replace them with a 25 percent share of *new* customers who are better than the old. The fear of loss through change is scary, but a successful executive has to come to grips with the evolution of business relationships.

THE IMPORTANCE OF SOLITUDE

To develop your maturity, you must detach yourself emotionally from your environment. You must do this while remaining warm, close, and humanistic to others. These two things are not contradictory; however, much time is necessary to acquire this balance. A top executive must seek solitude, but be extroverted. Solitude helps an executive be comfortable with himself or herself. Solitude helps put your life into perspective, and sorts out all the information that impacts you. Extroversion and maintaining warm relationships with your people are important, and a basic personality trait of many executives. Executives must genuinely like to deal and work with other people to reach their goals. Learn to empathize with people, but not to sympathize with them.

One of my favorite client-presidents has beautiful social skills. To all practical purposes, he appears to be extroverted. Charming, humorous, and a good listener. On profiling him, however, I realized that he is truly an introvert who has learned to be an extrovert because it makes business sense. He laughingly agrees with this.

During a business meeting, he commented to me that he bought a boat. I asked him how large it was, and he said it would hold about 10 people. I responded that it would be great to take a bunch of people out fishing. He told me that the object of boating was not to see how many people he could get in the boat, but how many he could leave on shore. He further explained that solitude on the water was better than a visit to a mental health counselor because of the insights solitude gave him.

As a former mental health counselor, I agree with his wisdom. People go to counselors to help them sort out their problems. Mental health counselors help their clients see, understand, and accept truths. Through solitude, one can see truths in a deeper, more personal, and more meaningful way. I find in my consulting that senior executives are usually very fond of time alone, and try to experience solitude whenever possible. Solitude helps your unconscious communicate or "align" with your conscious. Alignment is the key to inner awareness. Quality alone time releases repressed material into your consciousness, and helps you become aware of how you really feel about issues.

All executives should seek alone time every week. You can't do this at the office, but on your own. With the demands of living, family, and the community, executives often cheat themselves out of their alone time. My advice is: don't. Try to find 15 minutes of solitude a day to reflect upon life.

I never could figure out why my father used to like to barbecue so much. Even in freezing weather, he would stand out with his grill all by himself in the darkness. Now that I'm older, I find I like to barbecue, too. It's the only chance I have to be completely alone! Everyone seeks solitude.

MATURITY THROUGH DETACHMENT

The most important mindset of the executive is a detached attitude. By definition, this is a psychological separation from what is happening in your environment. Only through detachment can you function with objectivity and recognize truth when it is revealed. Detachment is not distancing; distancing is when you do not become close to others because of a fear of intimacy. Detachment is when you are unbiased, unprejudiced, impartial, and unemotional.

Keep a resolve that the outside world can't shape your perception of yourself. Detachment is a needed commodity for great decision making. It's also important for your self-perception. Top salesmen have known this for some time. They face more rejection in a week than most face in a year. Top salespeople have quiet recognition and appreciation of self. The very top people enjoy awards and monetary success, but their recognition of themselves is what drives them.

Resolve to be contented and peaceful, regardless of what happens in your business day. This attitude of detachment is acquired when you overcome the tendency to judge yourself and others. It is only through judgment that doubt and negativism begin. As odd as this may sound, detachment means you are indifferent as to success or failure. This way, equilibrium and an inner sense of peace is maintained. Forgo the glamour of public opinion, and begin to accept failure and glamour equally with no real emotional arousal from either. Don't become excited with success, and don't moan over failure. There is not as much difference between the two as we like to believe.

An entrepreneurial friend of mine developed a successful real estate firm, and grew very wealthy. Like so many other Texas businesspeople of the 1980s, he overleveraged himself. When real estate prices dropped dramatically, he went bankrupt. At lunch one day, I asked him how life was different now. He replied that there was very little difference between the two lifestyles in actuality; most of the differences were simply psychological. Each day, he got up and tried to make positive things happen, took care of problems. In the evenings, he went home, exercised, had dinner, went to bed. This was exactly his routine in life when he was rich.

As he said, business fortune and luck tend to ebb and flow, but our attitude toward life doesn't have to ebb and flow with it. Work for the joy of accomplishment and achievement. Hold no more admiration for yourself in victory or defeat. Success is to be pursued, but never pursued to the exclusion of spiritual growth and happiness. We all agree that money doesn't make us happy in the long run. The lack of it shouldn't have the opposite effect.

Competitive people—and so many executives are—obtain their self-esteem by ranking themselves against others. Victory over others is their driving force. I am advocating victory over self. When you're competitive and try to surpass others' achievements, your attitude becomes burdensome. For example, I've noticed that one of the differences between salespeople who achieve over the long haul and those two-year flash-in-the-pan types that all companies encounter is the ability not to get euphoric over successes, or overly disappointed about failures.

Realize that big deals make us emotional, but they bring only temporary satisfaction and momentary jubilation. When you are overly competitive, it drains your energy. It's not motivating. By being inwardly calm, and making your number one objective overcoming self, you can give maximum effort every day, and let success take care of itself. In the daily striving, find joy and inner peace.

A form of calmness to help put your life into perspective is meditation. This Far Eastern mental health balancing technique is rapidly catching on in our country. The science of meditation has been in existence for thousands of years, but only now is being popularized in the West. Meditation's purpose is growth through calmness and the focusing of energy. Through meditation, your mind's capacity to visualize is enhanced. In the West, we refer to meditation as quiet, reflective time. Millions of us seek this through fishing, gardening, hunting, painting, and other quiet, recreational activities. There is an inner urge to seek to disconnect with our consciousness, to explore our unconscious. We explore our unconscious to find a deeper understanding and intimate knowledge of ourselves.

By exploring our unconscious, we can recognize our inner intent and solve our problems. Quiet, reflective time gives us freedom because it inspires different options for solving our challenges. Our options are our freedom. A discussion of meditation is beyond the scope of this book. Excellent books on meditation can be found in the self-help section of your local library or bookstore.

MATURITY THROUGH DISCRIMINATION

Another way to intellectualize your emotions is through discrimination. By definition, *discrimination* is being able to visualize what the outcome of a decision would be by imagining the different options in a situation and then objectively choosing between the positive and negative.

Executives must be able to focus their minds externally to assess a situation, then focus internally to gain insight into that situation. At this point, through discrimination, intuition (Chapter 3) is free to begin. To intellectualize does not mean to repress. Discriminating is examining a situation independent of emotion. This is part of the discriminatory process. Through discrimination, you are able to define precisely to yourself where you stand and the pulls of opposites.

For example, in corporate America many people define success as being a prominent and powerful executive. But in the 1990s, it is increasingly important to be a team player. Executives want to be chosen as a leader. These two desires conflict: being a team player and being the team leader. There are no specific answers here; your answer must come from you and your value system in the situations into which you are thrown. However, when you tell yourself the truth it is easier to deal with these opposites. No matter how difficult the problem, through inner truth you find the single best solution.

Discrimination is the way to guard against deception. Quiet confidence and a constant search for the underlying motives of others' behavior and your own thinking process leads to clear thinking. Don't be suspicious, but have discrimination. Suspicion affects your attitude toward life. Suspicious people are never happy.

Suspicious people are correct in saying that there is evil in the world, and that one must be on guard. They are correct in saying there are evil people. But they tend to overgeneralize and have a constant skepticism. Suspicious people often have selfish hearts. They make lousy team players. They hold grudges. Suspiciousness, seen in its truer sense, is an inner anger. Suspicious people dwell on frustrations and are quick to see human frailties. A suspicious personality wins battles but ultimately loses the war. Suspicious people can't find joy through maturity.

All people with whom you come into contact have an effect on you, either good or negative. When we approach the world with trust and discrimination, we gain in maturity, grow spiritually, and draw good people to us. Sigmund Freud once said that we are placed on this earth to learn to work and love. We must learn to do both, for without these, we lead empty lives and die spiritually bankrupt. Control your emotions during work. Don't be a mean, grabbing, selfish monster and then expect to come home and be a warm, caring, happy person. The spheres of your life are connected and influence each other.

MATURITY THROUGH SILENCE

The mature executive is cognizant of the vital importance of his voice and the right use of words. Words, once said, take on a life of their own. They are difficult to retract. Mature executives understand the power of silence. They hold back their thoughts until they consider what they want to say. The purpose of speech is to make our thoughts available to others. Thought precedes the voice. Your words will either harmonize a situation or create problems. Your speech has more impact when you are silent until you have something important to say. Think before you speak. Silence is much better than the wrong words.

One president I consult to told me that a tremendous irritant to him is an executive who "needs a lot of air time." These types of executives tend not to be taken seriously in the long run, because when they mouth off about issues and rattle on, they tend to lose others' interest. Executives who need a lot of air time do not have emotional maturity and self-discipline.

Personalities collide in organizations. The emotionally mature executive, if involved in such a situation, can detach himself, at least emotionally, and take a more objective viewpoint by listening. If you're involved in an emotional situation, silence may do more to help resolve the problems than anything you can say. Executives who don't understand the power of silence set themselves up in the long term for a lower level of success. A talkative executive may win a battle, but she loses the war. The ability to be quiet and calm in the face of emotionally charged situations is one of the most pronounced characteristics of the mature executive.

Strive to have inner calmness. Wise people are calm people. Wisdom is based on the knowledge of when to speak and when to be silent. It is rare to blow a business deal, or get yourself into an emotionally difficult situation, by keeping your mouth shut.

BEING OPTIMISTIC

The mature executive has to look at the future with objectivity and optimism. Fear of the future is a blend of instinctual memory and anticipatory imagination. Few executives truly escape this mental health menace. Fear of the future particularly plagues marketing executives. Marketing and sales executives tend to be more emotional in nature. They are often creative, but have a harder time keeping a rein on their imaginations.

Marketing executives have a deep understanding of the fickleness of customers. Many customers treat salespeople and other marketing executives poorly. For example, they will not return phone calls. At the last second, they may renege on a done deal. They may delay decision making for no business reason but simply to demonstrate power to you and to themselves. Customers will keep salespeople waiting for no reason. They say when they will be available, and when the salesperson arrives for the appointment, the prospect is nowhere to be found. All of these things in combination lead to anticipatory fear.

Marketing executives, more than any other type of executive, must have continuous optimism. Often optimism is the only thing going. Believe there's a big deal around every corner, and that you're going to get it. You know there are going to be a lot of DFTs (deals falling through), but that can't slow you down.

Executives, like all people, get worried and anxious some of the time. Our sense of our own limitations and inadequacies can erode our confidence. It can be a long and protracted emotional strain carried over many years of living. Through correct discernment and a positive attitude we handle the strain—and grow from it.

Remember that fear grows as we pay attention to it. Fear doesn't exist until we think of it and make it real. Most of the hours spent in anxiety are illusions. Our worst-case scenario rarely comes into play. And even when it does, we can handle it.

Fear is reduced by internal peace and harmony. Then there is little difference between hot and cold business cycles. If you are internally happy and contented, external events don't determine your emotional state. On a personal level, we are afraid of our complicated lives. Complication brings oppression. When we are successful, we accumulate, and our possessions take on a life of their own, becoming burdens instead of rewards.

Recently, one of the most successful professional people I've ever met told me that he regrets his life. For most of his adult existence, he has been accumulating "stuff." Now, toward the end of his life, he regrets spending so many hours being afraid that he wouldn't achieve his goals and get all the material things he wanted.

Executives can also be afraid that they will wilt under the pressure of others' expectations. They want to impress their spouse, their spouse's family, their own family, members of the country club, their church, their social clubs. We all want the admiration and respect of our parents. But having great expectations of significant others creates anxiety.

Executives can fear that their power will be usurped, or that they'll be taken advantage of in a business deal. Executives' power is part of their identity, and when that power is threatened, their identity is threatened. We can fear that others will despise us, look down on us. We may fear that praise will be withdrawn. We can fear that opportunities will come and we will fail to see and grasp them. We can fear that we may fail to "make good," and so we have a play-it-safe attitude. These attitudes prevent us from taking risks, and so we're afraid that we won't make good again—a vicious cycle.

Finally, certain stresses and fears affect the entire office—other people's fears permeate us. Someone may have nothing to fear, but can learn to be afraid by identifying with someone who does. Disassociate yourself from others' reactions, and you won't absorb the poison of their negativity.

This seems to happen in sales divisions more than in other organizations. A top producer will pronounce the market to be soft. Those words become fact when others begin to fear that they, too, will be unsuccessful. The top producer's comment sets up the cycle of expectancy, confirming incidents that perpetuate and prolong the down cycle. Even in a depressed market, the difference between survival and being knocked out of the race is generally hard work with a healthy dose of optimism.

An executive must be optimistic, because when others sense resignation or pessimism, it affects their willingness to make a true, deep commitment to their work. Be a beacon of strength, not subject to the fears of others. Employees look to the executive as a barometer, and they react to what they see. The mature executive realizes this, and doesn't allow fear to penetrate his behavior.

Each day, our thoughts create forms. When we think harmoniously or correctly, we create a positive form for our lives. Destroy the forms and create a new reality if your form is negative. It is not so much fear of change that prevents people from developing, but fear of destroying the old form. As a beaten dog returns to its master, a beaten person returns to his or her negative thought process.

OVERCOMING DISCOURAGEMENT AND DEPRESSION

Discouragement is a result of a perceived incapacity to be adequate to the task laid out before you. When we begin to doubt our ability to overcome the challenges of our lives, discouragement sets in. Discouragement happens when our sense of proportion and balance are lost. Step back, view life objectively. Equilibrium is then reestablished. All things come to pass, and you can only do your best. Learning to discriminate between what you can control and what you can't control is the development of poise—that relaxed, in-control attitude so valuable in an executive.

Understand the value of your time. If you discriminate between the things you can do and things you can't do, you won't waste time trying to change the things you can't control. In the midst of profound difficulty and distress, the test of courage is to remain faithful to your set of ideals and strive to be optimistic.

Over the past 30 years, there has been much research and popular writing on overcoming discouragement and being optimistic. These writings reason that it is not the stressful situation that made you depressed or discouraged, but your attitude and beliefs *about* the stressful situation.

If you looked at 100 people before, during, and after a crisis, would you expect all of them to react the same way? Some would feel depressed or angry. But a percentage would view the event, after they got over the shock, as being the best thing that ever happened to them, an opportunity to make something else bigger and better happen. They would realize that depression is another form of selfishness. When you're depressed, you focus energy on yourself—you feel sorry for yourself. Situations have a life of their own. Often the *only* thing we can change in a negative situation is our attitude.

The *belief* that you can control your emotions leads to the *ability* to control your emotions and overcome depression. With depression—and all of us face it temporarily—use logic to see its causes. Then decide whether these causes lie within your own personality or if they're caused by the environment. Again, the challenge is for the logic to overcome the emotion, for the intellect to rule the emotions. Problems which appear overwhelming to you are manageable from another's objective viewpoint.

When I listen to executives express their problems within a corporation, and even in their personal lives, I'm struck by the fact that often these problems are merely inconveniences of life, and not the earth-shattering problems the executives perceive. When we begin to examine a situation emotionally, we're not aware that our personality is coloring the situation. We don't factor our high degree of emotionalism about the issue into our opinion. We accept our own opinion as factual truth. Once we do this, the emotion is now "truth" unalterable.

This is limiting. We are confused, but we can't understand why others in our environment view the situation in the world differently—"incorrectly." We don't understand why our boss is so stupid she can't see the obvious. Again, the boss is looking at the situation from a more objective—or at least different—viewpoint, often with additional information and without the emotional taint with which we view the situation. Our opinion is often composed of bias, slant, and uninformed prejudice.

Another cause of depression is acting in an unethical way; we become depressed when we have violated our perception of ourselves. On an unconscious level, we all realize the basic truth of the golden rule. What goes around, comes around. Business people who are unethical can make a fortune, but they never seem to be happy. These "successful" people are usually beset with problems as self-inflicted punishment for violating the golden rule.

Another practical payoff to good behavior is extra energy. Conduct yourself in a manner that is above reproach by your inner ethical standards. Your energy will not be wasted in an effort to justify or conceal your improper behavior.

Sometimes top executive team members will have an overwhelming drive for individual success. They want power and materialism, and their value systems or ethics are cast aside. When this thought is multiplied within an organization, the results are disastrous. There is usually some backbiting and power contests among the top executives. When this is carried to the extreme, however, no synergy develops, and the organization flounders. When ambition is ruled by lower-order needs or survival instincts, the ambition leads to unscrupulous behavior.

Individually, when you build your success, stay within your inner ethics—what you know to be right. Realize the impact that business decisions have on your self-opinion and self-esteem. Your business decisions are an outgrowth of your value system. Making a fortune by taking advantage of everybody you can will ultimately cause you unhappiness. The cost of psychological distress is high. Tension, irritability, and neediness are the result. "Making your numbers" in life is empty unless the process and aftereffects are fulfilling.

Success without mental health is not success. This fact is becoming more recognized with the materialism of the 1980s firmly behind us. In Texas in the early 1980s, oil and real estate were making people with moderate education and intelligence levels rich. Many could not psychologically handle their unearned good fortune. There was a popular bumper sticker which read, "He who has the most toys when he dies, wins." This bumper sticker is displayed by psychologically immature people. The evolved executive's bumper sticker would read, "He who has eliminated the need for toys in his life, wins."

Humility leads to happiness. Success without humility leads to stress. It's stressful to be worried about being respected. This is self-centered energy. When you begin to reach your goals, you have temporary happiness in your life, but your joy is short-lived when too many self-congratulations creep in. Remember happiness is when your goals are met, but joy is when you, as a person, reach self-realization. You will find joy when your value and respect for yourself are not contingent upon your worldly success.

Mentally healthy executives are a potent force in the world of business. Mentally balanced senior executives do a great deal of good for corporations and the world. Their employees' lives are enriched by being associated with them. They do a great job of stabilizing the company. Ultimately, this leads to a terrific bottom line. Employees gravitate toward mentally healthy executives. They make excellent mentors, and develop the ideals and value systems of their corporations. Maturity is the most sought-after executive commodity.

POWER GROWTH TIPS

1. Maturity is a global human quality that transcends all faiths, races, and regions.

2. The more you can overcome your survival instincts, the more evolved you are.

3. Gain insight into your need to be dominant.

4. Develop a sense of proportion as to your true contribution—have humility.

5. Crises produce a clearer vision.

6. Seek solitude to help your conscious gain insight into your unconscious. What you are unaware of greatly determines what motivates and directs you.

7. Learn to detach your ego from your people, yet remain close and humanistic.

8. Learn to reflect before you speak. Overcome the need to express yourself to reinforce your ego.

9. Embrace your vision with objective optimism.

Chapter 3

Power Intuition

HOW INTUITIVE ARE YOU?

In making a decision I believe in gathering all the facts first.
Never Seldom Sometimes Usually Always

When the facts don't support my feelings, I make my decision based on the facts.
Never Seldom Sometimes Usually Always

Once I make a decision, I never change my mind later because I feel uncomfortable with it.
Never Seldom Sometimes Usually Always

I reserve judgment about people until I get to know them.
Never Seldom Sometimes Usually Always

I don't like to make decisions without careful consideration.
Never Seldom Sometimes Usually Always

I can always rationally support any decision I make.
Never Seldom Sometimes Usually Always

I don't think I use an intuitive decision-making approach.
No Yes

If you circled more answers toward the right side of the page, you have a logical, deductive-reasoning style of decision making.

If you circled more answers toward the left side of the page, you have an intuitive approach to decision making.

We are concerned in this chapter with the art of balancing logical reasoning with intuition in gathering and assessing information for business decisions. Throughout our formal education we receive instructions on following guidelines. We are taught methodologies to study and acquire information. This creates the basis for deductive reasoning. Through study and effort we build a reservoir of knowledge that can be used for higher levels of awareness than simple memorization.

The ultimate expression of deductive reasoning is intuition. More and more in the coming decades, successful business executives will allow their intuition to complement their logical understanding. For many years, the world of business has been the world of intellect. Intuition as a business tool has not been given enough credence in traditional business school training. It will be increasingly necessary in the years to come that you, the reader, find a way to honor your intuition, the feelings and insights received from your higher consciousness. The strictly scientific, intellectual approach expands your field of awareness, but this expansion constitutes a prison of limitation without intuition.

Executives are paid to make difficult decisions. I'm not talking about assembly-line or administrative decisions; at that level, industry doesn't really need people who think abstractly as much as it needs people to perform tasks correctly. It is easier to make a decision based on numbers or follow a prescribed process than it is to make a decision based on complex undefined values. As a top-level executive, you're called upon to make decisions relying not only on *objective* information (like numbers), but on *subjective* information—your feelings about how a situation will manifest. Your intuition takes into account those things which cannot be quantified.

When asked for the specific reason behind a decision, executives often respond with vague statements. This is especially so when regarding a difficult decision that could have taken a number of different directions. Executive-level decisions are often judgment calls. Which vendor should you go with? Which individual should you hire when two applicants appear equal? What new markets should your company penetrate? Should you merge with another company or not?

Should you give up trying to win that new customer or persist? Should you give turkeys or calendars for Christmas presents?

The executives' decision-making process is difficult to dissect. The process is outside their range of awareness. They don't bother trying to analyze the process; they simply defer to their intuition. Intuition, like many higher-level concepts, stubbornly refuses precise definition because the process is totally contained within each person; all we can do is to describe the meaning of the word as it relates to us. We will consider it the immediate flash of understanding, awareness, and synthesis of the totality or wholeness of an event.

Intuition can be compared to love. Intuition is to the mind what love is to the heart. Intuition is the direct perception of truth independent of any reasoning process. Intuition has been defined by some with descriptive words such as "holistic," "inner truth," "enlightenment," "pure reason," and "true reality." Every individual defines intuition differently because it's a process of feeling—the ability to feel the energy being projected by a situation. Intuition is not simply the result of recognizing similarities or having a clear, analytical mind. It is a comprehensive perception of the mind's *illumination,* which is the mind's highest use. Intuition is just knowing.

Intuition is spontaneous. It seems to come without an active effort on the part of the person feeling it. Reasoning, on the other hand, is the process of accumulating facts and making deductions based on those facts—a process which takes place over time with deliberate and sustained effort. Intuition allows you to look *beyond* the physical reality that is seen and heard to the subjective reality—the reality interpreted by your own consciousness.

Intuition is the *gestalt* of your thought processes and internal perceptions—a leap in reasoning based on many bits of information, but which reaches a conclusion beyond and greater than all those bits. To illustrate, here are examples of gestalt.

In music, each individual note makes a sound, but when all of the notes are put together, a tune emerges that is above and beyond the individual notes which comprise it. Pieces of a jigsaw puzzle when viewed separately make no sense, but when they're put together, they form a pattern or picture—the gestalt of the pieces. Intuition is a gestalt psychological process that occurs when your thoughts are distilled into a focused whole which breaks through to your conscious awareness. In a state of contemplation, ideas pass through our minds. Suddenly there is a flash of intuition. When the flash ends, the intellect takes over to process and interpret what has just been revealed.

At this point, we have a choice whether or not to act on our intuition. The specific steps are usually fairly obvious once the big picture, synthesized by intuition, occurs. Implementation is usually a process of carrying out those necessary steps that lead to action. Many people fall down at this stage because now is when the hard work begins!

Interestingly, when I looked at a popular psychological glossary and desk reference book, I found that intuition was not included or mentioned. The glossary defined *instinct,* however, as an "inborn drive." Primary human instincts reported included self-preservation, sexuality, and—according to some proponents—ego and social instincts. It appears easier to refer to and understand our lower-order instincts because they are more observable; they resemble those of animals. Psychologists base much of what they believe about humans on their research with animals. It is, of course, perfectly true that we *are* animals and share instincts with them. Although animals have intelligence, and certainly can learn, as human beings we don't associate intuition with animals; only instinct. Intuition appears to be accorded to the human species only.

Carl Jung, a psychiatrist and former disciple of Freud, considered instincts part of the "collective unconscious." Jung defined the collective unconscious as the aggregate of symbols, energies, ideas, forces, and feelings accumulated during the history of the human race. It is the psychological thread which links all humanity. The collective unconscious has been described as a psychic sea that surrounds and influences everyone. This collective unconscious has been built up over millennia, and is given or placed within each one of us at birth. The collective unconscious is all the inherited predispositions a person brings into life. The predisposition to believe in a god is an example. As proof of the existence of the collective unconscious, human beings in most cultures recognize and acknowledge the existence of a force greater than themselves. This is the psychological thread that connects us all.

Sensitive, mature, intuitive executives tune in to the collective unconscious and are guided as to the true big picture. Although they might not be aware of the concept, they are still very much guided by it. We will not digress too much into Jung's theory of the collective unconscious. However, the subject is well worth the reader's time and energy to delve into because Jung's ideas help explain how a person can develop his or her potential, what holds him or her back, and how to overcome forces previously unrecognized by personality theorists.

Intuition is connected and similar to lower kinds of instinct and is a product of evolution. For example, the instinct of the migratory flights of birds is demonstrated in people who have a great sense of direction. A higher level of instinct occurs when a person says "I have a gut feeling," indicating that in their solar plexus region they have registered a sensation that indicates something, although they have a hard time articulating it.

One can be physically instinctual, as in basketball or golf, and have a natural shot or swing. Some athletes have much higher instinctual court or field awareness—they know where everybody is and what their next movement is liable to be. Another instinct, the herd instinct, evolved from wanting safety and security. Even today, typically, people feel more secure in their opinions if they see that other people share similar opinions. As dangerous as society is, we prefer being around others rather than being alone. Successful and intuitive executives know that introducing the right set of energies will lead to higher team cohesion when people connect with others of a similar vibration. The final evolution of the herd instinct is internationalism and a sense of universal brotherhood. This outcome is already beginning to be seen. The growth of the power of the United Nations, the easing of the arms race, the global economy, all have as a basis the herd instinct.

Another instinct is sex, which stems from the fear of separateness and loneliness. Pain avoidance and wanting to be physically comfortable has led to the field of medicine. Dominant behavior, encountered often in the corporate world, comes from the fear of death; it is the instinct of self-preservation.

A client of mine, Jody, has some very dominant traits. She studied the videos of air crashes on television to determine the safest seating position in the plane. She noticed that when planes broke in half, the seats over the wing section remained intact. When the top was ripped off an airplane, the people over the wings were never sucked out. So she sits over the wing when she flies and watches the flaps to determine whether or not they're in the correct position for takeoff.

One time, Jody thought the flaps were not properly positioned for takeoff. She signaled for the flight attendant. "I'm sure the pilot knows how to use the flaps properly," the attendant assured her. Jody insisted that the flight attendant contact the pilot immediately. "Those flaps are not in the position I'm accustomed to seeing them in." People were starting to stare at Jody.

The pilot patiently explained that on this particular model of aircraft, the flaps weren't raised completely before takeoff. "I was embarrassed, of course," Jody told me later. "But if I had it to do over again, I'd still ask," she laughed.

This instinct of self-preservation led to a belief in an afterlife, an important aspect of religion. Now, religion is evolving to spirituality, the recognition that God is not apart or separate from a person, but that a person is a part of God.

Intuition comes from the instinct of inquiry. Education and the acquisition of knowledge for its own sake is the natural evolution of this instinct. Through experience and the building of general information, you create a growing reservoir of thought you can tap into for still further and higher intuitive experiences. Consciousness is a fountain which has no limits. For example, people have more opinions than they have read or heard. It is an intuitive process when they make immediate connections and form opinions about areas that they have not had previous training or knowledge of but are only presented information about. When you are asked for your opinion, you dip into your reservoir of consciousness for a reply. Recognize there already exists a relative degree of synthesis in your consciousness. With every thought you contribute to this pool or synthesis and provide a larger pool to link up with; thus consciousness seeks to expand. Energy, when transformed into a higher state, seeks perpetuation.

Intuition is a divine gift that is inherently ours but much of intuition's potential is not manifested because we are not cognizant or aware enough of our physical sensations. We need to better apprehend our reactions to information and learn to trust our reactions. Intuition is a *feeling,* and you need to be physically in touch with yourself to exist more at that level of sensitive awareness. We cannot learn intuition as we learn other skills. People can be shown principles which seem to help people become more aware of their bodily reactions. However, intuition must be largely self-taught and recognized personally. This higher-level mental processing can only be developed gradually.

The ability to know higher-order truth is latent within each of us, capable of fuller existence. Most of us only use our intuition occasionally. Imagine what you would be like if you existed in a constant intuitive state. The gradual recognition of your intuition is a signal of transformation to greater maturity, a critical link to your personal and professional growth. A goal for you is an increased ability to perceive the thoughts and feelings of others—this is a sign of increased intuition. Intuitive management is being aware of the world of subtle phenomena, beyond the observable. Within the gross form of reality lies a subtler form which we can only contact with acute perception. The subjective world is more real than the objective world. This is simple and straightforward to those who (intuitively!) accept the truth of this statement. It is just as obscure for others who require replication or justification.

When we become sensitive to unrecognized forces, we see fundamental truths of life. When we hear truth, our intuition speaks to us with directness and clarity to confirm what we are hearing. When one of your advisors tells you to do something, and your intuition goes against what he or she is telling you, you have a strong tendency not to interpret those recommendations as truth. Over time, we should pay attention to our intuition because we realize that when we do, we operate on a higher plane. Our intuition becomes the new reality in our life, and we change. For example, former accountants, now high-level chief executive officers, have told me that numbers used to be the basis of their reality. Now intuition is, and numbers only serve to enhance and reinforce what they know to be true.

COMMON SENSE

Intuition has been called a high level of common sense. Common sense can be viewed as the fusion of the senses: sight, sound, touch, taste, and smell. When all of these sensations merge into one, they give an overall impression: intuition. We've all heard the statement, "Common sense is not common." We shouldn't expect it to be. The other physical senses are not evenly distributed among individuals either. Keenness of sight ranges from big-league batting champions to those who are completely blind. Hearing acuteness ranges from symphony conductors to those who are profoundly deaf. Human beings demonstrate the same variety in their degree of common sense.

Being intuitive allows you to identify the subtlety of personality reactions. The person with common sense reads people well and predicts the outcome of situations well. Others with a great deal of "knowledge" are blind to even the patently obvious. Psychologists have more recently embraced what has been the rule in business for years: *people with good social skills do quite well in life*. Until recently, intelligence tests have not really measured social sense, timing, manners, or the ability to be a good, general conversationalist. Obviously, some people have *very little* social sense. They walk away from a conversation or group meeting and have no real idea of what went on. People without social common sense seem a bit odd, and are commonly referred to as "nerds." Their hair may be too long or too short—never in step with the current style. Their clothes are never quite right. These people are often amazingly talented in other areas, but in the social arena they do not excel.

As most people have *some* talent for music, most people have *some* common sense. As a society, however, we tend not to admire people with a great deal of common sense as much as we admire talented artists, writers, scientists or athletes. However, people with a common-sense approach to life do exceptionally well, both in management and in other spheres of human activity. People who can fuse all their senses and then follow their intuition are truly gifted—as gifted as any professional athlete or musician.

Former U.S. President Ronald Reagan approached the world with a common-sense perspective. His detractors constantly pointed to his relatively poor intellectual ability compared to other high-level executives and government officials. But there he was, holding the top job in the top country in the world. Here is a man who understands common sense, and who relies heavily on his intuition. He realized early in life that the microscopic analysis of numbers was best left to the intellectuals who consider numbers reality. After listening to the intellectuals, he focused on his internal awareness of truth as he saw it.

To trust your intuition, and the decisions based on it, you need positive self-esteem. Ronald Reagan has positive self-esteem—he is secure in his own identity. His presidency is long over and his critics remain, but few dispute the point that Ronald Reagan has gone a long way in life on his intuitive skill.

If you have been on a managerial team, you know that doubters make lousy team players, and seem not to exhibit common sense in social gatherings. Habitual skepticism means all new information is filtered through this screening process. Skeptics only hear the negative. They will claim that they are playing the devil's advocate in order to get people to see all points of view. Again, in certain cases this may be true and even warranted. In many cases, the cynical person simply wants to show his intellectual prowess, gain self-esteem by "winning" a disagreement in front of his peers, etc.

People can focus too much energy in one specific area, thus becoming highly knowledgeable, but lacking in the ability to see the bigger picture. These individuals and everyone around them realize their inability to be a *true* leader. These types need to move from being theoretical and intellectual to being practical and effective. They are wasting time simply because of the illusion of their ego. People with true constructive doubt do not prejudge or judge too quickly, but try to verify what they are being told based on their own experience. The trick is to walk the fine line between gullible belief and inherent skepticism. The number of people adhering to a belief doesn't guarantee its validity. Don't accept ideas just because they have won popular approval. Approach situations with intellect coupled with an optimistic, discerning spirit. Do not approach situations without conviction and passion. Without these emotions, nothing worthwhile ever gets done. A passion implies intensity, an outreaching of the mind. The leader's passion must stop short of fanaticism, which is an unreasonable zeal bordering on frenzy. Fanaticism is a compensation for a hidden, unconscious doubt.

True intuition is always practical. An executive's decisions must be eminently practical; this is of primary importance. Executives must have a practical understanding and a capacity to see clearly and understand correctly. The true basis of executive competence is practical intuitive decision making due to correct experience which is stored accurately in the executive's long-term memory. Intuitive executives realize and accept that their job is to assess and deduce the nature, quality, and level of energy behind the outward form that is observed. A person who is intuitive knows truth and understands more than the person whose knowledge is derived from mere book learning and dry intellectual discourses.

The prediction of the future is another quality of the higher conscious. People who are in touch with themselves have powers that we consider psychic. That is one of the reasons that peaceful, mature people have common sense. Peaceful individuals exhibit sound judgment, which is the ability to examine several situations, see the relationships and possible outcomes, and choose the correct one.

Evolved people gradually are put into positions of subjectivity because of their ability to rely on inner thought. Mature executives are wise, and wisdom implies sensing impermanence. Everything changes, nothing remains the same. When they try to explain their internal abstract thinking, words fail them and veil the deeper meaning of what they are trying to accomplish. Therefore, there is increased isolation when you move up to the level where you get paid for accuracy in your subjectivity of impression. It is difficult to explain all of the finer points of your reasoning so that people understand your vision of where you want the company to go and how you want to get there.

CONNECTING DECISIONS

Intuition is a form of creativity. Creative people see analogies, they see links in a relationship that *already inherently exists.* There is no separateness and all things depend on cohesion for their existence. Nothing exists independently; everything exists because of something else. A simple example in the world of business is sales. The sales process obviously does not exist by itself. There must be a product via operations, accounting, recruiting, etc. Otherwise, sales has nothing to sell. When you stop to ponder the subject, nothing is isolated; everything exists because of the force and action of something else. Thus there is a subtle thread that connects all things. This thread is both actual (in the sense that all tangible things are built on the structure of the atom) and psychological in the sense that all phenomena exist because of consciousness. If we did not have awareness, nothing would exist.

Creative people feel, sense, and recognize these inherent relationships; with a flash of insight, they recognize the connection. Their minds reveal to them associations between two apparently different and distinct concepts. Their wisdom is seeing the connections. Their perception is unique and reveals what the rational mind (using testimonial, inference, and deduction) cannot reveal. They see the underlying *causes,* not just the *effects. Causes* are more difficult to understand—and understanding causes is an insight of intuition. Causes produce effects; the two are easy to transpose. Effects are the result of energy which has come before. Much of our daily activity is handling the effects of energy, the cause of which we don't completely understand. In business it's often called "putting out fires." You are really putting out effects because you can't see or understand the causes or you are not in a position to change the causes. Most people have a classical mindset of cause leads to effect. This is dichotomous, dualistic thinking. Wisdom and creativity allow us to see combinations and realize connections. Cause and effect are indivisible, and the intuitive mind knows this.

Intuition allows executives to be multidimensional. It would be great if we could understand all facets of a situation in depth, and then make a decision. But that requires either an incredibly high IQ or a lot of time. The truth is, we *can't* know all the dynamics that constitute a situation, but through intuition—even if the situation is not fully understood—a good decision can be made. If executives took the time to understand completely all the information presented to them, the rest of their careers and their businesses would suffer too much. Executives, by definition, *must* be intuitive, and feel comfortable identifying themselves as such.

The masses mostly look at events as isolated and individual. Seeing events in isolation is a form of ignorance. The extent of this ignorance varies from person to person and causes many problems in business. Examples abound—people see the customer as outside and distinct from the company, not realizing that the customer is a part of your company, for without the customer you cease to exist. This form of ignorance promotes territoriality in companies. People do not recognize that their departments are not separate units, but are part of the whole. They define their job and their role by their job description. Union members refuse to do important tasks because it's not in their job description or union contract.

Many companies go to a great deal of time and trouble to develop highly accurate job descriptions and analysis based on the rational thinking that you can't evaluate someone unless you can measure that person against a common standard and set of objectives. Although this approach has merit, it would be so much better to instill group consciousness within the employee and add on-the-job analysis secondarily.

One time I went to dinner with a company president to a quality restaurant which was very popular. We had to wait in line 45 minutes just to be seated—this was probably tough on my dinner companion. He owned nine restaurants in a chain which was doing reasonably well, but nothing compared to this 15-unit chain. (His restaurant, right across the street, was 40 percent full—doing poorly, considering it was a Friday night.) We were finally seated and ordered our meals. They arrived within an acceptable time and we both enjoyed our selections.

Halfway through the meal, my glass of iced tea needed refilling. A waitperson saw my empty glass out of the corner of his eye. He swiftly came over and saw that my glass was refilled. My dinner companion, the restaurant president, pulled at the waitperson's arm and asked him, "What section of the restaurant are you responsible for? Which are your tables?" The waitperson replied, "Sir, we have a set of tables that are our responsibility, but *all* of the tables in the restaurant are our *main* responsibility." My friend turned to me and asked, "George, how can we develop that kind of thinking in our chain—how do we train people to have that orientation?"

It was a good question—one that continues to grow in importance. Industry in America has slowly come to the realization that morale and desire for excellence is critical to corporate success. Leaders have realized that myopic thinking causes the setting of artificial boundaries, and descriptions cause poor communication.

The executive must show through analogy and specific example how each part of the company is dependent upon all other parts, and that all employees are loyal to the collective ideals for which the company stands. For this abstract concept, reference and reinforcement to concrete examples during meetings, in newsletters, and through other communication forums are critical. In order to instill the team consciousness that my dinner companion wanted so desperately, there has to be an orientation toward the previously mentioned metaphysical truth: nothing exists without being dependent on other things for existence. I am told by people that I am lucky to run my own company—how nice it would be to be independent. Nothing, of course, is farther from the truth. Independence is an illusion, an impossibility. I am completely dependent on my clients, my profession of management consulting which I certainly did not create but only am a part of, the overall economy, the level of modern thinking among executives who potentially hire a person such as me, and so on.

The executive has to handle conflict, complexity, and uncertainty on a daily basis and must feel comfortable with a short job description stated in general terms. The higher one goes in a corporation, the more ill-defined and ill-structured the situation is and should be. The top 10 percent of the general population is more skilled at handling jigsaw problems that call for seeing how discrepant parts fit, or can fit, together. Uncertainty, by definition, is a situation that is variable, changeable, unpredictable, and only encompassing partial knowledge. As one company president told me, "Dr. Watts, I have a problem that I want your opinion on. I know only half of my advertising works; the problem is, which half?" The more knowledge-based jobs, such as those of the technician, can be described in great accuracy so that performance criteria can be clearly established and monitored with precision. But the executive's job is to figure out which half of the advertising works or some similar challenge. A challenge could be as open as "given the skills and knowledge of our labor force, what new business should we be looking at or getting into?" Or, "Should we try to find a suitable company that would make sense for us to acquire where the synergy would really be worth it?" It takes a broad thinker to respond to these examples.

Some executives, a dying breed, handle a lack of structure by simply ignoring the parts that cause anxiety. For example, sales lacks structure. It can have some outline of structure in the sense of having so many calls to make or contacts to be established; but the key variable, the other human being to be contacted and sold to, is unpredictable. Thus, only the general aggregate is predictable. Every day and every encounter is different. Some executives simply refuse to place themselves in this uncertain environment by pretending that they are too busy with more important matters than talking to customers. Even if your job does not directly involve dealing with customers, your job must ultimately be linked conceptually to making the customer satisfied.

The executive's job obviously includes decision making and problem solving. Decision making deals primarily with evaluating and choosing from a set of alternatives. Problem solving is more complex and requires an accurate definition of a situation, development of alternatives, and then a choice of the path to optimal success. Both decision making and problem solving require judgment.

Three parts are always involved. First is the *type* of decision that must be made. For example, executives have to hire and fire people, decide to go with one marketing campaign or another, or decide how to structure the organization for optimal efficiency. These types range from fairly routine to critical.

The second aspect or part to decision making is to acknowledge and factor in the organization's *climate* and *culture*. Some organizations have a policy of not laying off people in slow times unless absolutely necessary. Others, particularly companies built on deal making (i.e., buying a whole company by financing), lay people off as part of their strategy from the word go. Companies that are basically run by financiers who buy and sell companies, or people who want to start and build a company fast in order to sell it, generally breed the culture that doesn't develop loyalty. This is not to say that the company isn't profitable, or that people won't work hard. But there is a sense of impermanence; everybody acknowledges to themselves that given a better opportunity, they would leave that afternoon. Executives come and go, staying only a year or two. All decisions are handled at the top and people are as expendable as equipment. The person at the top is generally very smart and shrewd and gets what he or she wants. The employees aren't stupid, however; they understand perfectly well that the owner(s) don't really care about them as people. The employees know that they are only useful in how they can further the company owner's goals in life. It's a bargain—time for money with little sense of belonging. The top people or owners can talk a good speech about how "quality is a team effort," "our biggest asset is our dedicated people," etc., but the only reason the people perform to a quality standard is because they were raised to be proud of their work and to be proud of their profession. It is these concepts they are loyal to, not the company.

This sense of climate or culture is like living in a neighborhood whose members have a sense of pride in their lawns and everybody's house looks nice. Nobody really knows each other and this is all right; there is a sense of pride in who you are. Nobody expects to know anybody else, there is little sense of community except for the mutual interest of what houses are selling and for how much. Another neighborhood may have an identical type of person who possesses a sense of pride, but the neighborhood also sponsors block parties, neighborhood crime watches, and "drive slowly because of children in the neighborhood" signs. Both are successful developments, but given a choice, most people will prefer the second neighborhood. Even if they start to make more money, they would rather add on a room than move because they like their living arrangement and realize that not every neighborhood has this sense of community. A close-knit, humanistic company is like the second neighborhood.

There is an obvious difference between these two cultures and this difference affects a person's decision making. In the first type of company, people tend to make short-term decisions that are self-serving. After all, why should a person take the long term into account when he or she won't be there all that long anyway? Also, the bosses are strictly in the situation to serve their own needs, so why not play the same game of selfishness? The second company decision makers take a different view. They want to make sure that any decision they make won't be hurting another person or department. They try to learn more about the different facets of the organization and are more willing to help another executive, etc. Their decision making is long term (i.e., they want to add on a room and not move!)

Organizations' climates differ in other ways that affect decision making too. One may have defined its market well, its customer base well, and stays in its niche, while another company is still trying to understand itself, its market, and is more willing to define itself loosely. One culture may be conservative and require many signatures and sign-offs before committing. Others, very decentralized, allow the person at the scene to go with what she thinks is best. One company is generous with its resources, others are tighter than the bark on a tree. Decision makers have to think carefully and thoroughly about the milieu they are in and what the ramifications of their decisions might be.

The third aspect of decision making is the *decision maker herself*. This is the only element under your personal control. What kind of person is the decision maker—impulsive or reflective, compromising or uncompromising, self-sufficient or team-oriented, authoritarian or democratic? How dogmatic or close-minded? Dogmatic people want and demand universal, single truths that they apply to life. (Facts about yourself come slowly; we are all a little dogmatic and myopic when it comes to understanding ourselves.) Does the decision maker like to be proactive and make things happen, or just reactionary, preferring to be safe and collect data and wait for the ideal time? How has the decision maker previously handled similar problems, and how has that experience influenced perceptions? How much does the decision maker really understand and know about the problem? How smart is the decision maker? How motivated is the decision maker to make a decision? Maybe it's easier simply to say no to everything that even remotely looks like it could fail. I've known people to even repress negative information so they won't know a problem exists, hoping the need to make a decision will go away. Maybe if they simply stonewall it long enough the problem will disappear or shift to somebody else.

When you constantly repress ideas, you become numb to the fact that you are repressing enlightening information and your vision is narrowed. We tend to distrust those concepts that our intelligence and emotional maturity cannot grasp. Narrow-mindedness becomes a self-imposed amnesia. Ideas are withdrawn from the table, never to be resurrected. This can often be because of painful experiences and impressions stemming clear back from childhood.

For example, the decision to implement a management training program is often challenged by some intellectually oriented executives. Training rarely is important to the intellectual because management training evokes emotions—how people should be motivated, how people need to listen for feelings being expressed, etc. Intellectuals would sooner not be reminded that they are perceived as unapproachable or distant from others. After all, they are constantly told by their spouses that they don't have the capacity to be romantic or to feel! Training is psychologically uncomfortable. They repress the real reason, disliking having to be put into touch with the emotional aspects of themselves, so they reject training because "the process is too expensive," or "it takes people off their jobs too much."

Repressed experiences, often stemming from childhood, affect individual business judgment/decision making in many subtle ways. Through repression, people become narrow-minded and negate information and ideas that would help them grow in their abilities. They seek to prevent their inner voice from speaking to their consciousness. They would just as soon not know what they deeply, truly feel. This lack of growth is dearly paid for by limiting their career and most of all their personal happiness. The inner voice is the voice of a fuller life, and of a higher and greater consciousness. Your inner voice causes conflict initially. It causes you to have to confront yourself more deeply. Even if what you believe in and behave like is admirable, you constantly need to open your mind up to your inner voice. You don't become better if you don't.

People have different levels of aspiration which affect decision making. How far do you want to go in life? Usually people have some kind of standard, an agreement they have made with themselves that they will obtain a certain level or achieve a certain set of goals in life and on the job. Their decisions tend to be made in relation with this internal standard or definition of success.

In summary, all three of these variables—the *type* of decision, the *climate* to be considered, and the *individual personality* of the decision maker—interact to result in the decision process.

PROCESSES OF DECISION MAKING

In many organizations, particularly large ones, decisions are made as much as possible by standard operating procedures; there is nothing wrong with this for routine decisions. But the executive doesn't make routine decisions too often, or else he or she would be called a manager. The next level of abstraction above a standard operating procedure is a *heuristic* procedure. *Heuristic* means a set of guidelines to find a solution. We all employ heuristics, or rules of thumb, to some extent to solve our problems. For example, when selecting personnel who have to interact with the public, the human resource director interviews by asking questions that help identify if the applicant is extroverted and has good social skills. He or she employs a heuristic model. A general rule of thumb for assessing people is to ask them a series of questions as to their social orientation, analyze their answers as a whole, then ask yourself if you cared for the person. Also to be observed are behavior, the tone of voice, the leaning forward of the body, the ability for the applicant to make eye contact, etc.

People are known to try to establish heuristics or general rules of thumb even though these general rules aren't warranted. People like to lay a form on their environment because it gives them a set of anchors with which to approach life. For example, take the roll of a die. There is a one-in-six chance that a roll will come up on a certain number, say four. Let's say you rolled three fours in a row. One would think that there is less of a possibility that you would roll a four again because you just rolled three fours in a row. But this isn't true; there is still one chance in six that you will roll a four again. The executives who try to identify patterns instead of going quickly with the flow, or who figure that two events are or are not connected, may be setting themselves up for migraines. Much of the time there is not a model you can fit an idea into, or a set of guidelines to which you can refer. This is what an executive gets paid the big bucks for—to make intuitive decisions.

An upgrade from a heuristic model is a linear model, derived from statistics. This is when the decision maker assigns weights to scores or attributes of a situation to predict the outcome. For example, let's say an individual applies for a job. The application process involves taking an employment test to assess verbal and mathematical abilities. Then the applicant is interviewed and answers to interview questions are put on a scale to compare how these answers stack up against successful people currently performing the job. Then the applicant's background data is examined—for example, how many years of college, how long did the applicant stay in a previous job, etc. All of these variables are assigned a numerical weight to indicate how one applicant stood in relation to other applicants. The numbers are added up to find a total score, which will help determine employability. This process takes some of the subjectivity out of the decision-making process. Benjamin Franklin used a variation of this technique when he divided a piece of paper in half and wrote "pro" on one side and "con" on the other and assessed the pros and cons of a situation to arrive at a decision. If he saw a condition on one side of the column which he felt was equal to a condition on the other side he would eliminate both, thus simplifying the final amount of information he had to take into consideration. Another similar model is a matrix used to identify the key dimensions of a solution, allowing the decision maker to take each dimension and place a value on it to help set priorities.

Most executives try to reason the likelihood of an event to transpire, a subjective ratio of probability. They rapidly mentally test many hypotheses and vary the factors as they do so, processing considerable data quickly to make a decision to a situation that needs a rapid response. Another more involved technique called "Delphi" advocates individual opinions synthesized into a "group think" to reduce ambiguity. The decision maker isolates his staff members from one another and asks them pertinent questions to get their individual opinions without the influence and interaction of other members of the team. After this has been accomplished, the individuals meet collectively as a group, each individual analysis is presented, and the best information from each opinion is consolidated into a whole. The best parts of each are combined into a group statement or position.

FORMAL DECISION-MAKING STRATEGIES

- Try to make decisions intellectual, cognitive, and rational to eliminate personal bias, which distorts information. Emotional decision making places the decision maker in a posture where he or she experiences avoidance, crisis management, and fire fighting in the long run.
- Try to compute the amount of uncertainty compared to what is known to be true.
- Decide what *is* or *is not* part of the problem
- Gather sufficient information, identify key dimensions of the problem, and structure the information so that it makes sense.
- Assess which factors you can control and which you can't, and what is important compared with what is not.
- Identify the priorities of the preferred solution. In this sense, you look forward and backward, define what

it is you desire, and work backwards to define each step that would have to be true for the goal to be accomplished.

- Allocate the amount of resources needed so a good idea doesn't go bad because of a lack of infrastructure.

THE SCIENTIFIC APPROACH TO DECISION MAKING

Intuition is not reputable in the world of science, which demands external proof. Intuition is generally recognized by the layman as a capacity of the human being. But since science is based on tangible fact, intuition has not received as much scientific analysis as have observable phenomena. This is beginning to change, particularly with the dissatisfaction of traditional psychology, which has not lived up to expectations. The growing new age movement, which essentially advocates that people identify with their own souls, is an example of a reaction to the failure of psychology to take the higher nature of man into consideration when solving one's difficulties and seeing truth.

Certain theories in psychology, particularly the field of psychology called behaviorism, deal with effects produced by the subjective life. Behaviorism is more concerned with what is measurable than theorizing about what may have caused the particular behavior. An axiom of science is "if it exists, it can be measured." The new age movement teaches that the individual, as a person, can intuitively measure the development of his or her consciousness. It is not necessary, or even particularly desirable, to subject this to outside measurement. Why? For whom? An objective measure is to quantify for others. But what of the persons who feel it more important to validate life as they see it internally, without having to prove what they know to others?

Western science attempts to logically reduce everything to basic elements which can be measured and predicted. Intellectuals believe wholeheartedly in the power of reason.

The scientist insists upon subjecting explanations of phenomena to controlled empirical tests. The scientist attempts not to have her belief system, which may be biased, mislead her. *Scientists try to own their belief systems and not have their belief systems own them.* Because of the difficulty of changing a belief, the belief possesses us more than we possess the belief. Here's an example—"I believe competition brings out the best in people." A competitive businessperson believes in this statement because of a belief in the inherent value of competition. Even when presented with evidence that *cooperation* brings out the best in people, he will still hold to his original belief. In our day-to-day living, we accept what we feel to be true, and it is very difficult to change. Thus, the belief owns us because try as we might (and we don't try very hard because our self-identity is partially composed of statements that we consider true), we cling to our thinking.

Science is built on the assumption that phenomena exist and can be measured independently of our thinking. The scientific approach dictum is that findings should be replicated so that conclusions from two different people are the same, and the results speak for themselves. To preclude a belief system from owning a person, the scientist sets up a condition called the *null hypothesis,* which means "none" or "no." A null hypothesis is a relational proposition. The assumption is that there is *no* relationship between two variables. The purpose of the experiment is to *disprove* the null hypothesis, thus giving evidence that the two variables in question *do* have a relationship.

For example, our earlier statement can be stated in a null hypothesis form: "Competition has no effect on the level of achievement." To test this statement we would have to define what we mean by "competition," and what we mean by "level of achievement." Then we would find two fairly identical sales offices in a company. In one office we could post the sales made by each individual salesperson. The top five people out of 20 in the office would receive bonuses, which would be a percentage of the gross sales for which they were directly responsible. Each person would be judged solely on the basis of his or her production; there would be no reason to develop a team consciousness.

The second office would take a different tactic. Here, only the office sales are posted collectively, individuals are told of their performances but competition isn't deliberately created. If the team makes its numbers, then everyone gets a bonus. The higher producers still get a proportionally bigger share, but unless the entire team makes the office's goal, only the top five people get their bonuses and these bonuses will only be 50 percent of what they would have been if the *team* had won.

Thus two opposing conditions are set up. The first office sets up a competitive situation where the individual relies solely on his or her own effort with little care how the person next to him does. There is little need for team dynamics because they are like 20 separate entities with no overlap. They simply have to get along well enough (i.e., don't talk too loudly on the phone, don't tie up the computer all day, make a fresh pot of coffee if you drank the last cup, etc.). The second office sets up a different set of dynamics. In this case, everybody wants everyone to do well. There is no open competition; a rising tide will lift *all* ships. People are rewarded for being open about their prospecting tips, more inclined to share some business if they can't handle it—after all, *somebody* getting the commission is better than *nobody* getting it.

Which office do you think would pull out ahead over the long haul? If you were a top producing salesperson, which office would you want to work in? What if you made the same amount of money under either system?

As an executive who would have to set up the compensation for all the salespeople, what scenario appeals to you the most and why? How about if you highly favored the team approach, yet I showed you convincing data that the individual competition format is best? Would you change your management philosophy? Would you change how you ran your office? Would you choose basically to run it by the numbers? Or would you say to yourself "I know open competition is a good way to motivate salespeople who are competitive anyway. But I also know that competition breeds distrust, even contempt, and creates an ultimately negative environment. We may sacrifice a little money along the way, but I believe that in order to build a network of offices sharing the same philosophy and value system, I cannot and will not create offices that have as their basic operating procedure a non-team-oriented atmosphere. We wouldn't have the synergy and family feeling that's important to me."

Now flip the coin over and look at it from the viewpoint of an entrepreneur who might be thinking, "This is a 10-year deal for me. I need to pump up some big numbers, keep expenses at a bare-bones minimum, open offices just as quickly as I can, and sell this company to a cash-rich buyer and retire to the Bahamas. I don't really care about creating a family feeling. Business means money, pure and simple."

Obviously in the above examples there is no right answer. That's why so many kinds of businesses exist that have different approaches, management styles, etc., yet are successful in light of the value system of the top people who own or run the company. The idea that there is a single management style, or there is a single value system or decision-making style that is correct is obviously wrong. It is far more important that, as individuals, we look into our hearts and define our value systems, our ideals, and what we want out of life. Then decision making will become relatively painless and easy.

The scientific approach can be a useful way of approaching the world because the scientific mindset helps eliminate the illusions created by emotions. This is contrary to how most people approach life. They think that something is true and seek to find examples to prove it. Their emotional bias causes them to distort the environment and selectively see those events that confirm their opinion. The null hypothesis was created to keep the researcher's bias from affecting the experiment the same way people's biases affect their views of life. Science doubts; it doubts what is purported to be true unless it is systematically verified under multiple conditions. Executives do not experiment (i.e., manipulate phenomena in order to see which scenario works best). They go by their intuition through experience learned over time. They react to situations, handling several events simultaneously. There are no experimental conditions; they are concerned with the total environment, not just a part of it. Our test subjects are our employees, our customers and ultimately ourselves. It is the hopes, disappointment, fears, joys, mistakes, and achievements that provide us with our basic backdrop of decision making.

Your investigation of truth must begin afresh in each case, for each situation is unique. The solution is not completely derivable from any preconceived formula. At best, you have a hypothesis, but be prepared to drop all of your arguments for the sole purpose of discerning truth. Your value system is your guide. Keep some of the philosophy of the scientist, because an extremely important component of a good decision is eliminating the emotional orientation and viewing the event dispassionately.

Intuitive perception comes from within, knowledge comes from without. You understand from within. Intuitive persons know what to do and have no second thoughts. They see a direct path; it is a simplistic yet accurate appraisal. In most circumstances, simplicity has the advantage over complexity, but executives have to understand when the simple way is not the way of truth. Intuition is the line of least resistance which invariably presents the solution with elegant simplicity. The truer something is, the faster it takes effect. There is an exact understanding of purpose and direction, and the energy is parsimonious. Through being mentally attuned, intuitive persons *know* when their decisions are right. They do not *react to*, but *respond to*. Reaction is more automatic; response implies a more cognitive, higher use of the mind.

Experience teaches decision making. Here is a story I once heard at a conference. A young, newly hired woman came in to talk to the president and founder of a successful organization. She sat down, and after some initial talk, the president asked what was on her mind. "Ms. President, can you tell me how you made it? I mean, how did you achieve all your success?" The president looked away for a minute and then said slowly, "I can answer your questions in just two words: right decisions." The young woman nodded her head in agreement and then replied, "I can appreciate that, Ms. President. But tell me, how do you learn to make right decisions?" The president smiled and said "By making the wrong decisions." You must be willing occasionally to make the wrong decisions in order to gain the background to make quality decisions on a regular basis.

THE NUMBER CRUNCHERS

Most new M.B.As and Ph.D.s are intrigued with numbers. They like to crunch them, analyze them, and argue about them. Experienced executives like numbers too. The difference is experienced executives use numbers to justify the course of action to which their intuition leads them. When you look within, you become accurately subjective. You realize that facts are not as much help in selecting the right course of action as intuition.

Senior executives are given many scenarios based on numbers. Numbers are a *version* of the facts; they contain *some* usable truth. The number crunchers tell the truth attractively from their perspective and interests. Nothing is more common than attractive numerical projections—especially when the presenter wants your money.

At the vice presidential level, many people flow through the office offering suggestions and solutions to problems. (As I've said before, the higher you go in the corporate world, the more advice you get!) By having the inner calmness that leads to wisdom, executives begin to know truth. They become sage, wise, and nonjudgmental. Out of the information from all the advisors, the quietness of truth is revealed.

Executives realize that numbers which produce overwhelming evidence for one conclusion can—with the push of a button—be made to support another conclusion. The decision to use one vendor over another may produce very different results, even though numerically the vendors look the same. When the decision maker has to choose one, intuition decides the matter. Subjective impressions are the way deals are made.

The accountant-type personality always focuses on the bottom line. Bottom-line results are easy to measure and observe. Focusing on the bottom line is of considerably less value than focusing on your internal awareness of what is causing those numbers and deciding what action to take. Executives don't need to be number crunchers; recording and describing the numbers is the role of the accountant. The executive's job is to understand intuitively what to do about the numbers. The executive is responsible for creating the energies that drive those numbers. The numbers exist because the executive has put ideas into physical form—the result of action taken.

In practice, executives use numbers to evaluate others' performance. On an individual level, we tend not to measure ourselves, but intuitively assess our degree of success and failure. When evaluating our progress, we glance at numbers, but our ongoing awareness and feeling about what we're doing is the reason for taking action. On occasion, we may evaluate ourselves numerically, but this is used only to verify our own intuitive self-evaluation.

If you have a set of numbers that conflicts with your intuition, do you change your mind as a result of the numbers, or do you hold steadfast in your conviction? If you felt that you were on the right track, but the numbers showed that you were doing poorly, would you change tracks, or keep on in the same direction? Most of us with a deeper level of confidence would stay on the same track. Our decisions would be weighted against our past history of success. This capacity to weigh evidence, make decisions wisely, and accept only that which is compatible with one's intuition is characteristic of the mature executive.

Several years ago, I was on a committee charged with designing a new sign for a large real estate company. Our job was to establish a company image, and then work with an advertising firm to come up with a sign that would enhance our image in the community. We consulted several market studies which rated us on a number of variables, but the major force in our decision was intuition. I was uncomfortable with the fact that we had no demonstrable, logical reason to choose one sign over another. After studying the executive decision-making process for years, I learned that going with our intuition to choose the sign was the best decision mechanism we could have used. Incidentally, the sign change was extremely effective.

The facts about a situation are of secondary importance to our ability to reflect on the causes of what we know to be true based on our own experience. Sometimes this contradicts the current thinking or goes against what everybody "knows" to be true. Going against what everybody knows to be true happened to me professionally about eight years ago. Many professors of psychology feel that graphology—handwriting analysis—is worthless. Numerically oriented academicians dismiss graphology because studies have not proved it to be valid. Yet graphology exists and is enjoying increased use. The number of American companies using graphology is rising dramatically, and up to 85 percent of European companies are using graphology to help them decide whether or not to hire or promote a person. Articles and books on the subject abound. Yet when I was going to graduate school, I was told curtly that there was no validity to graphology, and the entire subject was dismissed without examination. I have been told the same thing at numerous professional conventions as well. I believed what I was told about the "facts" behind graphology for many years. The measurable facts in academic psychology show that graphology is useless. Several fortunate experiences caused me to reexamine my set of beliefs. Now that I've intensely studied graphology for a number of years, I can say to myself in truth that graphology is an excellent method of helping to ascertain a person's unconscious personality. Since the unconscious seems to defy measurement and is highly individualized, graphology does not lend itself to the traditional statistical analysis upon which Western psychology is based. However, based upon my own experience, I realize that graphology is valid, and can be helpful in understanding an executive's personality and management style. My intuition told me, after my own handwriting had been analyzed by a professional graphologist, that there was real truth in what I was told.

I had a choice to make: accept what I had been told by "knowledgeable" experts, or go with what I knew to be true based on my own experience. Executives are often given contradictory information by more than one "knowledgeable" expert. An old joke about economists is that if you laid them all end to end they still wouldn't reach a conclusion. Business executives are paid to reach conclusions.

THE PHILOSOPHIES OF EAST AND WEST

Western thought advocates seeking outside counsel. Outside counsel, when listened to, is unquestionably very useful. Eastern thought is more reliant on the inner voice, trusting in the principle that knowledge is important, but true wisdom is found within. Your primary source of gathering wisdom is with you all of the time. Your primary mentor is your higher self. It is important never to underestimate the abilities of your higher self, or the knowledge that your higher self has gained through working and living.

New age writers and Eastern philosophers suggest that intuition is an inborn drive. Intuition comes from a person's superconscious, whereas instinct comes from a person's unconscious. Our unconscious can't be seen or measured, yet psychology has shown that the unconscious is the basis of much of our behavior. Dreams emanate from the unconscious and give us insight into our truer motives, fears, and aspirations. Just because we are not consciously aware of something doesn't mean it doesn't exist and influence us. Intuition emanates from our superconscious, a uniquely human part of the mind that cannot be seen.

Intuition, conceptually, is more connected with the Eastern philosophies of life. Eastern philosophy tends to be more holistic. The East teaches that a creative energy force has given us all the knowledge necessary. We are to look within ourselves, within our superconscious, for the answers to our questions. The superconscious is our spiritualism, our love aspect—kindness, honesty, and courage all emanate from it. Intuition, or pure truth, comes from our *superconscious*. The *unconscious* part of a person's mind is the byproduct of lower-order desires. Both are instinctual; both can move us. By gaining insight into your unconscious and your superconscious, you can let your superconscious move you in the *right* direction.

Executives who have achieved high-level personality integration are in touch with their superconscious. The challenge is to tap into our superconscious, where intuitive decision-making exists. We must figure out how to align our levels of consciousness.

In the Eastern tradition, religion and intuition are both considered parts of the whole spectrum of existence. Spiritualism and the attainment of higher consciousness is the primary underlying goal of education. Paramhansa Yogananda, the great Indian philosopher, mystic, and teacher, dedicated his life to bringing the Eastern concept of yoga meditation and enlightenment to America. His theme was the fusion of Eastern and Western philosophy. He felt that the two patterns of thought and two ways of approaching the world could be molded into one, which would be more evolved, peaceful, balanced, and productive.

Contrary to the gestalt, intuitive approach of the East, our Western education advocates structure, empiricism, and mathematical or statistical validity. In the West, we value willpower in bringing our ideas into fruition. Our credo in business is "a sense of urgency." We want to fulfill our desired result of business—materialism. There is virtually no attempt to teach intuition in businesses, schools, or even in psychology departments. Intuition defies measurement and supposedly can't be taught. Because you can't see it, touch it, or taste it, it is viewed with skepticism, even suspicion.

Our Western continuing education programs for businesspeople stress objectivity. Investigation and knowledge come from the instructor to the students. We train the intellect by transferring knowledge. Our Western world demands that our intuition be supported by intellect before we take action. We recognize that intuition, in and of itself, doesn't net anything. All intuition does is indicate a distinct possibility. Our Western world is the world of action. At the decision point, our self-confidence begins to desert us and we doubt or overlook our intuition. We analyze it, we fear it is not logical, and we don't use it.

Looking back, when we've doubted our intuition, we've been *wrong*. How many times have you said to yourself, "I *knew* I shouldn't have done that." Or, "Something told me that would happen; I wish I'd paid attention." High-level executives who have arrived at a state of maturity have learned to overcome the inclination to doubt their intuition. Self-confidence gives you the ability to trust your intuition.

Once your consciousness has been touched by your intuition, the situation takes on a different tone. All decisions, after the insight of intuition, are shaped by that insight. The quality of your decisions does not vary when you rely on your intuition. Your decision is always the result of the highest and best use of your abilities because the superconscious is the highest and best use of your mind. Even when we have an imperfect grasp of a situation, we learn to decide through our intuition. Once you learn to look at a situation clearly and have used your intuition, your decisions should be implemented with no regret. When we use our intuition in decision making, an inner calmness prevails. There is no second guessing or remorse about our decisions. Count on yourself to make the best decisions you can under the circumstances that present themselves.

The philosophy of the East and the science of the West are similar in one respect: they both seek truth. It is their *approaches* to truth that are different. The Easterner seeks truth through enlightenment; the Westerner seeks truth through replication. The Westerner wishes to define reality; the Easterner accepts the premise of there being no definition of reality. Until 15 or 20 years ago, most Westerners totally rejected the Eastern philosophy of life. This rejection was not based on knowledge, but on an emotional, prejudicial reaction. In the West, we still tend to think our way of perceiving reality is correct. As a general rule, we have a better physical standard of living and are more powerful militarily. It is a short step in our logic to assume that our businesspeople are also superior. After all, we produce much more of the goods and services consumed in the world through our management techniques.

The recent popularity of the New Age movement and the poignant example of Japanese business success is showing the viability of multicultural concepts. We are desperately trying to learn and understand Japanese production methods. Until the beginning of the 1970s, nobody really cared about Japanese business concepts. It didn't seem worth our time or effort to study them. Now, certain aspects of their methods and quality control have won widespread acceptance.

Other countries such as India and Tibet, not well known for their productivity, have more recently become known for what they've had for centuries: a high level of spiritualism. The new management philosophies are a combination of perceptions and culture. Newer management theorists have an appreciation for all approaches. Cultures can, and should, learn from each other. We need to learn Japanese quality techniques, remember our "can do" American spirit, and learn the Far Eastern ability to connect with the superconscious. Then the achievement drive of our Western world will evolve. Not only will we produce more by bringing out the inner motivations of people, we will enjoy our executive roles as never before.

Western business culture advocates competition. Our weak die; our strong prosper. Survival of the fittest is another name for capitalism. This economic theory sounds cold and cruel, but in actuality can be the greatest form of humanism. Our superconscious, the kindness and generosity of our hearts, is designed to moderate the survival-of-the-fittest thinking. The survival instinct is partially neutralized by our superconscious, and as our society evolves and grows, it will be continually more neutralized. Our goal is to lift all of humanity up. There is no fear that our jobs will be replaced or taken, as we realize that there is a never-ending cycle to technology and innovation which will constantly create new and more interesting ways to make a living.

Our system of capitalism is a great economic force, not due to Darwinism in business, but due to mankind's innate humanism. As people, we intuitively realize at some point what we've always been told: money doesn't buy happiness. In business, power doesn't buy happiness, either. Americans are competitive, and we are taught to try to be first. We want our companies and businesses to prosper. But most top executives I've dealt with regard their competitors as "friendly," and certainly don't want them to go bankrupt or to fall on hard times.

We search for happiness, with predictable results. We can only find joy when we learn to give to our fellow man and identify with a greater energy and spirit. Mature executives rise to the psychological challenges of finding and understanding what joy is. They learn that they must give from the heart to find the happiness they seek. When we realize this, we become mature executives, mentors, and teachers. We become the type of executives people seek out to discuss their ideas. Our executive ability becomes more evolved. Our listening skills improve dramatically. We learn not to judge others. We become the type of executive who can relate to all levels of people, not the type who wants to eat only in the executive dining room.

These changes don't occur because we read a management book that tells us to relate to and communicate with our employees. They happen because we realize, on a deeper level, that this is the only way we can know our business. By slowly accumulating information from the grass roots level, the executive is able to make the broad inferential leaps of thinking necessary for strategic thinking.

The evolved executive may become actively involved in a truly worthwhile cause. We don't become involved with these causes to sit on the board of directors or to get invited to the yearly ball and wear our tuxedos. Commitment to our jobs, giving to charity, and the quality of our parenting cannot be measured—it is demonstrated. As we grow and evolve, we wish to give of ourselves—our time, energy, and money—not only to help businesses become as profitable as they can, but to help society be the best and most evolved it can be.

When we lead by connecting with our superconscious, our employees begin to connect with theirs. The organization creates a collective superconscious where people make the right decisions because they intuitively know and understand the company's value system and mission statement philosophy. Our well-run corporations have a collective superconscious.

Consultants like myself get a positive feeling from such an organization merely by walking through the establishment.

In athletics, incoming troublemakers often stop making trouble when they join a championship team. They become enmeshed in the spirit of the new organization, and learn to overcome ego and selfish instincts which made them troublemakers on their former teams. Suddenly they adapt and make the best contribution of their careers. Their consciousness is elevated by the collective spirit of the team.

ENHANCING INTUITION

Your challenge is to tap into your intuition consistently enough to recognize when it's speaking to you. You must have enough self-confidence to believe and accept your intuition, and then take action based on it. Executives who are consistently intuitive and use their intuitive power to better their companies and the people around them show characteristics of the mature, evolved personality. New executives are more "centered"—they have fused their different levels of consciousness. This alignment and harmony leads to evolved intuition—wisdom.

Is intuition genetically endowed? Do some people have it and others don't? Or is intuition a nurturing or environmental issue? If a child is allowed to explore and understand life on her own terms instead of having it dictated to her, does she develop intuition as a young child and increase it with age? The genetic-versus-environmental debate, long a fixture in psychology and biology, is giving way to a more interactive explanation. The debate is moving toward a combined and integrated genetic/environmental explanation which encompasses addiction, weight problems, and even psychological traits such as introversion and extroversion.

For example, we know some people are born with a weight problem. But through willpower, they can overcome their genetic predisposition and develop great bodies. They must be willing to sacrifice by exercising more and eating less than other people, but if they are willing to make the sacrifice, they can overcome their problem. Can we make the same assumption about intuition? Through effort, can we increase our ability to be intuitive? I feel that the answer is yes.

Simply put, intuition is developed by subordinating your ego and focusing on feelings. When your ego is removed, what is left is reality which *isn't* filtered through your emotions. You do this by focusing your internal awareness on what you feel.

Develop calmness. Anger, anxiety and stress obviate intuition. When we harness and control our emotions, we begin consistently to understand and use our intuition. Most really good ideas don't happen on the job—busy work environments just don't foster calmness and tranquillity. Great ideas come when you're at home, at rest, pursuing a hobby, or engaged in some activity that has nothing to do with the situation you were pondering. You feel relaxed, at peace, in harmony with yourself—suddenly the intuitive insight manifests itself.

We've all had experiences like this. You're not thinking about the situation confounding you, and the answer comes to you seemingly without effort on your part. Our answers may not be in our conscious awareness, but by asking the right question, relaxing the mind, we receive communication from our superconscious. Through silence and allowing the mind freedom to work, you can see truer reality.

Both intuition and instinct are subject to control and enhancement through the intellectual mind. Through willpower, your mind can control your biology and psychology. We can learn to control our stress reactions and gain conscious control over our body temperature and respiration rate. We can control our bad habits and negative thoughts by exercising discipline over our behavior. Control is not repression. Some highly religious people dispense countless "shoulds." They quote religion freely. They consider sexual thoughts bad. They consider certain acts sins. These people have not risen above such thoughts, they have *repressed* them through guilt. They often compensate for their frustration by being irritable and narrow-minded. They develop overly serious personalities and approach life as something to be endured instead of a process to be lived in joy. Intuition is rarely encountered in these types—only adherence and conformance.

Intuition more frequently occurs when you have as little repressed information in your unconscious as possible. Put another way, if you know yourself well, you have less "garbage" in your unconscious blocking information from your superconscious. A critical point in developing your intuitive ability is when you can speak the truth earnestly to yourself without allowing your ego to get in the way or distort information. Intuition is always available, but not necessarily accessible. The more you distort truth, the more you repress your intuition. The more your interpretation of reality differs from actual reality, the less you consistently tap into your intuition. Being honest about your motives brings out the quieting response within you. When we hear information that is not congruent with our value system, and we are judgmental or prejudicial, we will only receive distorted intuition about that subject area. When we control or censor information about a situation, intuition can't manifest in that situation. Intuition is nonjudgmental. You must remove illusion in order to gain intuition.

Through quietness and contemplation, executives tap into their inner minds and superconscious, and know what needs to be done next. *Contemplation* is the reflective silence between two activities which evolves and erupts into intuition. Contemplation works with ideas, not physical forms. By contemplating each decision as if it will come into physical reality, we assess the quality of ideas. Before physical reality, there is the reality of the idea. View ideas as reality without physical form.

Stress management courses have a common theme: the quieting of the aroused survival instinct, what was called in the last decade the fight-or-flight phenomenon. Stress management courses encourage biofeedback, breathing exercises, meditation, and avoiding emotion-stimulating foods—those containing caffeine, sugar, and so forth—all of which tend to clutter the mind. A real benefit of relaxation training is intuition enhancement. Intuition implies concentration. Concentration focuses and reorients your energy. Random thoughts with a high dose of emotions are subjugated to your higher consciousness, which is more focused. Concentration is intellectual, not emotional. Our emotions usually dictate how we wish life to be. When we are intellectual and able to concentrate, we focus more deeply and fully on the problem at hand. Intuition doesn't occur if you only want it emotionally. It occurs with maturity. The cluttering of your mind with emotions cuts off your intuition.

Intuition is a visual process. Use your mind's eye. Imagine a certain situation, visualize each scenario the situation could manifest, and then allow your intuition to work. To develop your intuition, picture your situation as vividly as you can in all of its detail; sense all of its qualities and its emotional effects on you. An academic approach gets too intricate and misses the point. To intuit, you must focus on a broader picture, and not get mired in detail. If I ask you to "see" a misty mountaintop which overlooks a meadow in the springtime, all of us can visualize our version of this scene. In your mind's eye, you see the snow-capped mountains, the green meadows, and the brook that runs at the bottom. If I ask you as the regional sales vice president how you think your sales force will do next quarter, you "visualize" and reflect on each salesperson in the territory, estimate their potential, their territory's potential, add your management ability to the situation, and come back with your answer. This process is visual. You picture the components which make up the data, then arrive at your answer.

This process of visualizing in your mind's eye is the process of receiving intuition. Experience helps you visualize and gain intuition. When you have invested a lot of effort and time in some aspect of life, through difficult times and subsequent analysis you begin to see patterns. Through those patterns, you begin to gain experience, and visualize what the future may hold if you pursue a certain course of action. Through the pairing of patterns and memory, you learn what to avoid and what to incorporate. Throughout a business day, the constant pairing of patterns comes into our conscious awareness. We begin to discriminate different ideas and different trains of thought, and arrive at a solid conclusion. This is experience. We use our intuition to combine our past experience with future visualization so we can assess what we are being told now. We make decisions in the present based on these factors.

Recognize that intuition takes work. It can be promoted and developed with effort. Intuition does not occur often and with consistency in lazy people. You need aspiration before you can have inspiration. Work hard, contemplate deeply, speak truth, and find calmness, and intuition will be yours. The basic principle behind drawing higher-order enlightenment into your mind is that what you seek will be revealed when you are open and ready.

The following is a summary of thoughts and suggestions to enhance intuition.

1. Discover the spirit of inquiry. When everything you do is predictable year in and year out, you become settled in your ways of thinking and reacting. Forget what you've done and start afresh. Always be thinking of new ways to become unsettled in your thinking patterns. Being dynamic means destroying. You must destroy your thoughts and veil of illusion. Be ever aware to the possibility of error and distortions; constantly try to keep an open mind. The more controlled you are, the less intuitive inspiration you will feel. Imagination is reached by an informal and unstructured mode of reasoning. Listen to your "inner voice" with

openness. Challenge yourself; why do you believe in what you believe?

2. Maintain inner integrity—have peace within. Honesty and sincerity of thought lead to the development of intuition. Inspiration (the inbreathing of an idea from a higher influence) comes with a sincere interest in what you are doing.

3. Visualization is the creative power of imagination plus mental energy. Look beyond your immediate goals to what you finally aim to accomplish. Let those anchors relay to you the information needed. Affirm and visualize as you say "I will do," and see the goal completed before you. You get what you ask for. But don't talk about what you are going to do; simply do it. Premature speech destroys things before they are realized.

4. When you are involved in a meeting, pay attention not only to the words you are hearing, but also to the feelings you are having in your body. Ask yourself, "What am I feeling when I hear this speaker's words?" It is through becoming aware of our feelings that we access higher reasoning. It is a facility that takes place over time. Intuition is the art of responsiveness to phenomena—in essence, the art of registering. The clearer, the more sensitive, and the more deeply apprehending your capacity to register the impression to which you are subjected, the more easily your superconscious speaks to you. When you are going to meet a person for the first time, or when driving to a customer's office for the first time, practice intuition by trying to visualize what the customer will be like, what kind of office the customer might have. Intuit what customers are going to say. What kind of mood will they be in?

5. When you persistently fall under the spell of glamour, your vision becomes fogged and misty. Pride causes distortion. Don't take your ego too seriously! Qualities such as honesty and truth, integrity and humility help you channel energy more effectively. When wisdom increases,

ignorance decreases. Only through the speaking of truth is wisdom developed. Truth is progressively revealed; what is seen as a fact eventually is seen to be but a fragment of the whole. Then, what is perceived to be whole is eventually seen to be only a portion.

6. Selfishness affects receptivity to impression from other sources. The intense concentration upon the moods of the lower self is a form of selfishness. Don't be so concerned with how your ego is feeling. The purer your motive, the more you develop intuition. Being centered gives you clarity. The less you constantly consider your own thoughts and are able to concentrate on others (not to judge), the better able you are to receive truths. Truth is susceptible to many interpretations, but the more you have detachment from desire and emotions, the more purely it is revealed. We create mixed messages to ourselves and others when we rationalize our behavior and thoughts. Do not gloss over faults or excuse yourself. Learn to diagnose and call things by their true names.

7. Overcome the foreground of daily life. Realize that what you are experiencing is only the outer layer of energy. There is another level of subjective energy that is more real. The foreground is the stress that is close by, directly in front of you. Adjust your perception so that the minute-to-minute, hour-to-hour and day-to-day stresses don't drain you of energy and deplete your resources emotionally. The noise must fade into the background. Calmness gives you the hidden power to overcome the obstacles in your life. Being calm makes you more able to achieve success. The constant activation of adrenaline in your body, over a period of time, conditions your body to perceive that feeling tense and uptight seems natural. We tend to forget what it is like to feel totally relaxed. We believe that to feel anxious is desirable and natural, especially at work. Some feel it gives them an edge. Naturally there must be enough stress on you to motivate you to take action. If you are so "relaxed" that you

are lethargic, you will have little stimulation for effort. But bear in mind that calmness is your more natural state and is your true nature.

POWER INTUITION TIPS

1. Your intuition is your highest use of your mind and comes from within.
2. Intuition stems from the instinct of inquiry—be curious about life.
3. Everything is connected—creativity is the seeing of the inherent connection that is already there for you to discover.
4. Intuition allows you to be multidimensional.
5. True confidence is acknowledging and acting on your intuition.
6. Calmness allows your mind to recognize intuition—stress obviates intuition.
7. Intuition is primarily a visual process. Visualize in your mind's eye.
8. Intuition takes practice and work.

Chapter 4

Power Leaders

Choosing management as a career is a great personal decision. Responsibility for the welfare of employees and their families is an honor not to be taken lightly or cavalierly. Upper-level executives have chosen a profession in which they achieve through other people.

WHAT DRIVES PEOPLE TO BE EXECUTIVES

In Chapter 2, we read that executives often have the drive for power—the need for dominance. Personality assessment defines this as the need to direct, control, and convince others. Dominant people have a need to control their environments, including the other people in those environments. This control inhibits creativity in their teams. They delegate, but they don't ever really relinquish authority—they're always looking over shoulders and correcting. Their subordinates can't develop a sense of ownership or pride. Recent management theory focuses on empowerment, but unless an executive has worked through her need for dominance, empowerment is just another catchphrase, never put into practice.

One of my favorite clients, a 70-year-old CEO, told me, "The only thing I can say about power is that I would rather have it than not." He comes from the *new* school. Although his statement suggests power is important, it is assigned a secondary position. Too many executives think of it as a priority. The "power is all" philosophy worked back when employees stayed with a company until they got their gold watches on retirement and were happy just to feed their families. But this is a new time; top professionals have many options open to them, and our corporations fiercely compete for the top producers. You must attract and retain top producers for *your* team. An executive who relies on power to manage is playing the new game by the old rules—and he is going to lose.

In some conservative, stagnant companies, a bright and dominating person will still find a way up the corporate ladder. But these traditional organizations that look to the past for their answers will have difficulty staying in business in today's competitive global marketplace.

Today's successful executive is an empowered servant who leads by facilitating. The "need to manage," a popular expression some years ago, was essentially referring to the need to dominate. Our innate need to *produce* should be the primary drive of business. We dominate in an attempt to *force* that production to occur. But we can produce much more by synthesizing our teams and instilling harmony in group dynamics. Dominating the group to fulfill power needs isn't motivating.

During this century, the average citizen has evolved toward independence and freedom. The more evolved people are, the more they crave this feeling. In the future, our employees will want even more independence and control. As an executive, you must be able to give freedom to your subordinates to accomplish their goals without undue influence. The value of the individual must be a cornerstone of your beliefs.

When I first got into management, the old-school dictum recommended one executive for every eight managers. This ratio has changed dramatically: executives now commonly have up to 20 managers reporting to them. Executives no longer have time to demand and evaluate in-depth reports. They don't spend hours and hours in meetings to maintain control. Managers are expected to be more self-managed, and as their executive, you're going to have to grant them the freedom to self-manage and make decisions instead of handling everything yourself.

Controlling executives are organizationally destructive. Motivated by an unconscious fear, they compete against the world. They are manipulative and interfering, not facilitating. They control by refusing to release any decision-making power. Under stress, these executives are rude and irritable.

Aggressiveness is usually a double-edged sword. Though a dominant attitude can quickly produce results, it also produces other less desirable effects. For example, dominant corporate executives are not mentors; they do not foster leadership qualities in their subordinates. When I meet with these types, they laughingly agree that they have big egos. Aggressive executives receive lots of feedback from employees and consultants on how they need to change. They feel little, if any, need to change what they consider an effective philosophy and lifestyle. They do so little introspection that they never really arrive at the point where they feel an urge to create a change.

Watch for this type of executive. You'll see them on teams where a psychologically weak president wants dominating, tough-minded people to tackle situations he or she is too weak to deal with. Weak presidents are happy to give away all the power to aggressive, power-hungry VPs—as long as they don't have to dirty their hands or handle conflict.

THE POWER EQUATION

Personal power is a function of singleness of purpose and lack of impediments. Unless that singleness of purpose is constructed with a higher-order value system above the desire for control, it will be a one-pointed, negative energy. An executive who's totally out for status and power can wreak havoc on an organization. Potent personalities thrive in any field of endeavor where human beings gather ready to commit emotionally to an ideal. Potent personalities can manifest in the form of an Adolf Hitler or a pope. When such potent personalities are motivated only by desire, the organizations they run will eventually weaken.

How do you begin to temper your power need? First of all, don't interfere with any work that doesn't call for your attention. When you do interfere in these situations, you probably do so because of your ego need. Direct your employees' energy toward admiring the ideals for which the company stands. Don't strive to make your employees admire and focus on *you*. Have them focus on the vision of the company. Be dispassionate; don't allow excess pride to creep in and undermine your leadership style.

Beware of the *glamour* of being an upper-level executive. We tend to shoulder all final decisions in the belief that our people couldn't survive without us. When we examine the situation dispassionately, we find that the company can survive very well without us. In fact, decision making and performance often improves when the top executive doesn't have the final word. Pride and a sense of superiority produce a separate relationship between you and your people. Executives often feel that they are superior by endowment. Even if this is true, it makes little difference unless you use that gift to promote and develop others.

Be clear as to why you wish to be an upper-level executive. Our motives are generally infused with some unhealthy psychological needs which are difficult for us to admit. What quality is your inner motive?

Too many people desire management because of their inherent weaknesses, not strengths. They figure that the higher they go in management, the more secure their futures will be. Maybe they want leadership to enhance their self-esteem.

Righteous actions, especially if we draw attention to them, are rarely pure. This doesn't mean that the goals of those actions aren't valuable; they often are. The underlying motives are simply not as pure as the righteous lead themselves to believe.

Executives who are domineering want conformance. Conformance is a detriment. It leads to stagnation and a lack of creativity. People who like conformity like authority. The more you like authority, the more you look to your past for answers to your future. Many executives prefer subordinates who are obedient. They find comfort in dictating limitations and boundaries. They may even have a certain devotion to the company. But this energy is misguided. Dominant, conservative, conforming people are intolerant of other ideas and value systems. Their growth is limited by their fanaticism.

True leaders aspire to the leadership role to promote their ideas about their company. True leaders in today's world must free their actions and motivations from unhealthy influence from their egos.

I once met with a high-level executive to conduct a job analysis; I was interested in what he did and how he did it. The executive fixed me with a superior gaze and with obvious pride in his voice said, "I'm a leader of men." Unfortunately, his "men" under him felt he was a pompous jerk, and resented his air of superiority. He was fired about a year after our meeting. His explanation was that the president was intimidated by his superiority.

People who have fully matured have *worked through* their need for power. Focus on your vision, not on yourself. When you focus on your vision, your employees will do the same, and will put their hearts into their jobs. The only way your employees' higher consciousness can work is if they have control over the quality of their endeavors. Look at your employees engaged in a favorite sport or hobby to see how well they can produce when their hearts are in a job. Allow them mastery, and don't intercede unless you are needed. Allow employees to improve on ideas—their own *and* yours. Help them to develop their vision as much as possible.

Your challenge as an upper-level executive is to develop, focus, and emphasize the company's ideals daily. Humans have an inherent urge to create harmony and excellence in what they do. As an executive, it is your role to tap into this natural desire for excellence. When we see a picture frame unbalanced, we have a psychological need to balance it. People have a need to perform in some aspect of their lives with excellence. Don't train your employees to be good and obedient in carrying out your wishes. Teach them initiative. Teach them to become masters at what they do. Sure, suggest methods and techniques which have proven successful, but realize that most people are internally motivated to do things right, and they will—if given the opportunity.

Motivate your people to stand on their own feet, handle their own lives, and solve their own difficulties. Clear away impediments, and eliminate anything that prevents you or your people from achieving goals. The purity of your goals will show you what to eliminate and how to eliminate it. The more blocks you clear away, the more energy your people can focus on manifesting the vision.

Leaders are recognized by the influence they exert on their environment. Influence your environment by helping your people understand their objectives and priorities. Bring insight. Help them define the true nature of their problems. Empower your employees to feel that they can overcome obstacles. Help them feel capable of victory—it's a great motivator. When people honestly believe that with hard work their goals will be achieved, they'll work hard. Help your people feel victorious.

A true leader heals and develops other people's energies. Your energy awakens others' energy and brings their talents to the highest levels. Awaken your people's energy through enthusiasm—visible, positive energy. Enthusiastic people know that their optimism draws to them the energy needed to fulfill their goals. As a very successful vice president once told me, "It's much better to be a blind optimist than a 20/20 pessimist." Strive to make your style a combination of professionalism and enthusiasm.

EXHIBITING GOODWILL

Another important trait of the evolved executive is to be a trainer in the spirit of cooperative goodwill. At the higher levels of a corporation, you don't need to teach your people their jobs; they already know them. It's far more important for you to teach them a winning *attitude*. Top executives must exhibit goodwill by their own actions. Goodwill doesn't recognize boundaries and formalities. Offer spontaneous examples of goodwill toward customers and all levels of employees.

Vice presidents of marketing and top salespeople consistently tell me that the one internal department that screws up their deals by not showing goodwill is the legal department. Contracts should be simple and clear and, especially if service-oriented, based on goodwill. Most contracts for service industries are entirely too long if touched by the legal department. A joke in the sales force is that the legal department is the "sales prevention division." The legal department should have a relatively *minor* role in terms of power in a corporation. This goes against the grain of most attorneys' egos, but your profits will be much better if you follow this advice. Attorneys usually don't make goodwill or trust the basis of their contracts.

As an executive, lead with examples of interdepartmental goodwill, too. Cooperate with other members of the company even when they seem unreasonable. In addition to the benefits of demonstrating goodwill, this is usually the quickest way to defuse an unreasonable attitude. It is an emotional and maturational challenge to rise above the pettiness and divisiveness of your people, but immature executives can't be good team players. You must show your staff how to be good team players by being one yourself.

The chief financial officer of a food service company and I once went to dinner at a company-owned restaurant. When we arrived, he noticed some trash outside the entrance. He spent several minutes gathering it up himself, rather than simply going in and telling the manager about it. He was in charge of finance, not ground maintenance, but he realized that all employees are charged with forwarding the objectives and visions of the corporation, and acted on that belief.

Most religious ideals stress individual sacrifice for the good of the group. Our survival instincts impel us to strive for individual success and recognition. We must achieve a balance between being a strong, individual competitor and being a team player.

This balance is essential for success in team sports. Players must be aggressive to get on the starting lineup. Yet, interpersonal cooperation is critical to the team's success. Your job is to foster the creation of this critical balance in every team member. There is no simple, single formula to follow. You must examine your value system, your intuition, and your ideals to arrive at your solution.

A major job responsibility for an executive is to set ideals for the division. Ideals are a fusion of philosophies, strategies, and values. Ideals are the blueprint for ideas; they're a set of job specifications and goals. Evaluate ideas based on how close they can bring the company to the ideal. Then refine the ideas. When ideas agree with ideals, they are easy to sell.

Expect your people to contribute ideas to better the company, but don't expect them to measure those ideas against the ideals—that's *your* job. Ideas are as precious as water in a desert and mustn't be discouraged. Create an environment conducive to ideas. Hold the corporate goals steady in front of your employees. Remain objective, nonreactionary, and nonjudgmental. When you have an open, accepting, and encouraging attitude, ideas will flow forth from your managers. All ideas have error in them. There are no perfect conditions, no perfect solutions. Recognize the inevitability of error and factor it into your plans.

ACCURATE ASSESSMENT

An executive's job is to assess ideas accurately as they relate to the ideal. The executive must choose among options. This is why an executive holds a top-level position, and this is the value of experience. If your experience doesn't increase your ability to assess ideas accurately, it doesn't do you that much good. How do you ensure that your experience will increase your assessment abilities? Look for and be receptive to *true* feedback on your judgments and decisions.

In large organizations, employees often get inaccurate feedback. Those in sales get accurate feedback because there is direct profit-and-loss responsibility. Sales executives can usually see what works and what doesn't. In other divisions, we don't get such direct feedback, so our experiences are more challenging to assess objectively. Bottom-line responsibility helps us to remember our mistakes more clearly. With feedback, assessment abilities are enhanced.

Most managers who have held a position for more than 20 years consider themselves astute and polished businesspeople. But this may be an illusion if they don't get the feedback they need. The people around and under them often perceive them as bottlenecks of pettiness. They make the same mistakes over and over again. They see no reason to change their management style or approach to business. Over time, they become controlling and critical of things that aren't really important. They are busy, but not productive.

Departments without that bottom-line responsibility thrive under structures that provide little feedback. For example, an administrative vice president's job is to establish and monitor procedures so that the corporation's energy is the most productive. To be effective, he or she must understand this *real* role. The other employees are their customers, and the service they provide is reducing interference. Administrative work should be unobtrusive. Like many kinds of employees, it's often helpful to send administrative people out with salespeople to make calls—it reminds them what business is all about.

Another example of a division without built-in feedback is the legal department. They don't have bottom-line responsibility. Lawyers are trained to look at the world in a competitive, win-or-lose fashion. Some lawyers take this attitude with them when they leave the law firm and become head of the legal department within the corporate world. Business is seldom win or lose. Deals are lost and internal problems can arise because of the legal department's insistence on protecting the company. I recommend that these more rigid lawyers be trained in sales before being allowed to join the company legal department. They can also benefit from going along on sales calls. The goal is not to make them salespeople, but to help them realize where their services to the company fit in the bigger picture. Sometimes, the legal department views customers as adversaries. These professionals need to develop a high regard for the customer while protecting the company.

Here's my litmus test for a top executive. If you put one alone in a room with a phone and a phone book and tell him or her to make something happen, something does. Unfortunately, many executives in our corporations couldn't be successful under these circumstances. If a you want to be a top member of an executive team, you should be able to do the same thing. Most of us are trained to think of sales as a dirty word—we think of a pushy car salesman that may have gotten the best of us. Corporations need to be service- and sales-oriented to be successful. We need to sell our ideas internally and externally to be personally successful.

EXECUTIVES ARE TRAINERS

A top executive is a top trainer. Stress the value of becoming more educated and professional. Whenever possible, refer to or pass out articles of interest. Top executive people create dramatic professional growth for their people. The top executives I know are very proud that they've been mentors to others, and that their departments are asked to sacrifice their best people for other corporate opportunities. Realize that most people have something to offer if they're in the right position, given adequate training and management. By teaching and training our people, we develop our knowledge of our own jobs and ourselves.

Here's some advice that goes contrary to some popular management philosophies. Spend quality time with your employees outside the workday. Real teamwork is not created on the job; it's created after the job. I'm presently working with a company whose president feels that his team hasn't gelled, even though he's been there for four years. I asked him if the top executives ever got together outside staff meetings. He said, "No, we don't really like each other, and I really don't think we respect each other enough." My advice to him was to accept the responsibility of training himself to put the team in the position of being uncomfortable. People's defense mechanisms break down when they spend time outside the work environment. They begin to understand why others act the way they do. Then they begin to come up with quality ideas. The team now meets together occasionally after work or on Saturdays. They play golf or go fishing, but what they're really doing is developing the team. They're getting to know each other as human beings, not as executives. This adds the dimension of relationships we need to develop loyalty. We must establish bonds. The more you know people, the more confidence you place in the relationship.

KNOWING YOUR EXECUTIVE STYLE

Executives tend to think and reason in one of two ways. One is an intellectual or objective approach, and the second is through the heart, emotionally. Each of us uses a combination of the two styles, but one or the other will usually prevail. The objective, rational, reasoning-type executives want *ideas* for commitment and motivation. Emotional-type executives want *ideals,* and reference to ideals, for their stimulation and motivation. Which style prevails for you: your head or your heart? You must find the answer to understand and manage your motivations. Understanding your team members' styles is also critical, because each requires different techniques to motivate effectively and manage them. We will take an in-depth look at each style with several case examples which illustrate that *integration* of the two styles separates the top executives from the rest of the pack.

EMOTIONAL EXECUTIVES

Emotional executives look at the world through their hearts. They often have terrific interpersonal social skills, and are enjoyable to be with. Emotional executives are extroverted and interpersonally effective. They view the world subjectively, and judge situations from their visceral emotional reaction. Objective, quantitative facts are secondary to this inner evaluation.

These executives are attractive because they have zest and vibrancy. They often come from the marketing and sales division. They are used to selling their ideas, and intrinsically understand crowd or group mentality. Groups love to experience emotions. Emotions make them feel more alive, feel better about themselves, and feel more powerful. People enjoy being swayed by their emotions. The emotional executive appeals to their likes and gets them fired up about their dislikes.

Motivational speakers have an easy time getting simple emotional types excited. These speakers, however, have a much harder time swaying the intellectual-style people. Intellectuals may enjoy listening to a motivational speaker, but become bored rather quickly unless the material appeals to their mind, not their heart.

Emotional executives like to experience rather than understand. Understanding something in depth requires a great deal of technical study, and emotional executives don't have the patience for this. They work with and through others. Most often, they earn their credentials and validity within the organization by being a top producer. Their educational background usually is not a math or technical major. They channel their energies into verbally oriented pursuits.

Entrepreneurs are usually great salespeople. They understand how to make things happen, and can create deals in a relatively short period of time. Entrepreneurs have a vision—often rather melodramatic—like taking the company worldwide or being the biggest and best in whatever business they're in. They're entertaining and fun to work with. Group decisions, information sharing, structure, and feedback are forsaken in most entrepreneurial companies. These companies are run with a driving, pulsating, emotional beat. Those employees who believe in the vision and can cope with ambiguity and the top executive's emotional style stay and thrive. The intellectuals who can't get used to the craziness of the place leave.

Entrepreneurial companies move from crisis to crisis. They have a hard time getting on a smooth track. What is needed is emotional restraint—emotion balanced by intellectualism—but in an emotionally run company, the balance isn't always there. Emotional executives will cold-call for sales appointments even when they get out of sales and reach the executive ranks. More often than not, the decision makers they reach are emotional executives, too, and when two emotional executives get together, there is so much hype flying around it's hard to tell who's the buyer and who's the seller! Both enjoy the sales arena so much that the meeting becomes a stage on which they can demonstrate their sales skills.

Your company will thrive if you get these types into your sales department. Your role as an executive is to provide the balance. Get the salespeople to concentrate on generating logical, coherent, well-considered business plans. Get them to be more consistent in their analysis and study of the territory. Train them to use thought and reflection, and to investigate keenly all aspects of their business situations. Help them have a steady intellectual urge to explore issues. Salespeople usually are short on planning and long on action. Help salespeople to be wise, use patience, lay the groundwork, and consistently use formal decision-making analysis.

If you yourself are an emotional executive, use these same techniques to balance your life with objectivity. Remain extroverted, but develop your own center where you find isolation and peace. Try not to be so tuned in to others' energies; focus more on your own internal awareness. As an emotional executive, you are probably somewhat impulsive. You need to harness the power of mental discipline. Try not to become so quickly enthusiastic. Be more contemplative and detail-oriented.

Emotional executives are extremely intuitive by nature. As we saw in Chapter 3, when this intuition is refined and evolved, a dynamic executive emerges. When it is not evolved, however, intuition is manifested only occasionally. Thus, these executives rarely develop a smooth and steady style, and—worst of all, from their perspective—they turn people off emotionally because of their stop-and-start decision-making style.

Emotional executives must curtail their need for recognition and work hard for objectivity and restraint. Their main challenges are to learn to be comfortable alone and not to crave recognition. Emotional executives must concentrate instead of flitting from one idea to another so rapidly that they eventually lose ground and momentum by having to go back and finish what they should have done right the first time.

Emotional executives usually don't like computers, and meditation is considered out of their comfort zone. The emotional executive's personal checkbook is usually totally out of kilter. It doesn't make any difference, because that executive has lost it anyway. Initially, computers, meditation, and checkbook-balancing elicit discomfort in emotional executives, but by working through that discomfort, they harness the power of concentration—and then they're unstoppable.

Gary Dunham

A client company sent Gary Dunham to me to profile and asked me to render an opinion on whether he would make a good vice president of marketing. This good-sized firm had gone through several vice presidents over the past four years, and their last one was a total bomb.

I evaluated Gary and recommended him for the job. He has now been there four years, is earning good money. Both he and the company are doing well. The president tells me that when he retires in another five years, Gary may well be chosen to replace him.

Gary was young for the position; at 32, he was one of the youngest vice presidents I'd evaluated. Gary came from the sales division. He was extroverted, and had a natural ability to approach and deal with people. His strongest qualities are his energy and enthusiasm. He never seems to run out of energy. When he's not selling or managing salespeople, he's skiing, dirt biking, or some other strenuous activity.

On my profile, he said his strong points were that he was upbeat and a good communicator. He sets his goals high and doesn't give up. He's a fighter, and willing to fight for the right cause. He listed his negative qualities as "not adhering to procedure and being impulsive." Gary *is* impulsive and occasionally shoots from the hip. He can be a rebel without a cause. He needs to become more socially polished when under stress. He is sometimes forthright to the point of being blunt, an area that must be refined for him to succeed as a president. He certainly will have to become more diplomatic, and willing to engage in a consensus-building style, rather than selling everybody and railroading those who disagree with him.

From an emotional perspective, Gary is stable, perhaps on the tense side, but he maintains his equilibrium. He is a passionate human being with strong likes and dislikes. Once he has an idea or project going, he gets irritated if anyone interferes with him. He hates authority, and doesn't want any authority placed over him. He sometimes lets his pride get in the way of his decision making. He is, on occasion, somewhat of an egomaniac. Fortunately, he has the ego strength to give credit to other salespeople, and doesn't have to have the limelight *all* the time.

He is sincere and committed to his job. I also think he's very honest. He is a little immature in the sense that he's money-oriented, likes a lot of flash, drives an expensive automobile, and occasionally dresses in too bold a style.

He tends to make decisions too quickly based on his instinct, without mulling things over. With greater maturity, his intuition will take command, and he will learn to contemplate and make decisions from that contemplation. Right now, he is well compensated and enjoys his job, and his company finds his skills most satisfactory.

Marie Valdez

Marie Valdez is a partner in a large national accounting firm. She is 40 years old and in excellent physical shape. Well dressed and with a quick wit, she is charming. She was evaluated for the position of partner in charge of the management-consulting division. This division is the biggest profit center for the company and the head of the section was retiring. Marie had been a consistent top producer, a real "rainmaker" as far as bringing in business. In 1991, in a tough economy, she managed to bring in $1.8 million in revenue. She felt she deserved the top job in the division even though it would mean shifting her focus from selling to management. People were impressed with Marie, but there was some doubt as to whether she could make the jump from a big-time producer to management executive.

Testing revealed a very bright woman, falling in the 98th percentile in intelligence. She was just finishing her M.B.A. and doing very well. She had been married and divorced twice.

When I met Marie it was obvious she liked to be the center of the stage. She had a magnetic personality and a flair about her that compelled one to listen with interest. She felt her strong qualities were her intelligence, attractiveness, and dynamic approach. She felt her weak points were her directness and aggressiveness—she needed more tact. I agreed with her analysis. Marie did not really have as high a *need* for people as I would have surmised just by interviewing her. (Test results were 30th percentile regarding her need for people.) She was aggressive and dominant, easily able to *approach* people. She was uninhibited and could take the stress of being a selling professional. She signed her name in huge flowing letters with flourishes and underscored, indicating a strong social recognition need combined with independence. She was also very emotional and sensitive to criticism. She was a perfectionist and wanted things to be perfect in all spheres of her life. (I could see how she would be hard to be married to—it's tough to be perfect!) She had a tendency to handle her work herself because she wanted it done a certain way. She worked 14-hour days because of this.

In a social setting you couldn't compete with Marie. With her enthusiasm, confidence, and ability to articulate and express herself, she was engaging. She also had excellent listening skills if she thought you were worth listening to. If not, she would cut you off quickly. Marie had strong willpower. She grew up tough and learned to rely on herself. She would never give up. She also had street smarts and could get to the truth of the matter in a "New York minute."

I felt there was a strong potential executive inside that aggressive and emotional exterior. I recommended Marie for the job on the condition that she go to a psychologist friend of mine for 10 sessions and read five books on developing tact, diplomacy and leadership. Some psychologists are very good at giving a person feedback on how others perceive them and how they need to grow. I felt that Marie needed to get her need for attention under better control and have less of a need to be admired. Much of her aggressiveness was not so much wanting to dominate, but wanting recognition and not knowing how to get it. She needed to be humbled a bit, not enough to break her self-esteem, but enough to realize that other people need the limelight occasionally. She also had to grow a little and realize a good executive is not moody. She felt her moodiness was justified because of the revenue she pulled in. Top sales producers are sometimes allowed to be moody, but top managers cannot afford to be.

She was insulted when I gave my recommendations but wanted this job so badly she agreed. The psychologist did a terrific job and gave her insight as to how she was really being perceived. (Her superiors had a tendency to pull their punches in her performance reviews because they did not want her to be emotionally reactive—and she was the top producer in her six-state region.) She also went on a 10-day survivalist training trip where she was put into a forest and forced to be alone with herself for five days. She came out 15 pounds lighter and the worse for wear, but with a deeper understanding of who she was.

When I recently had lunch with Marie, I was delighted to find a much calmer, more grounded person. Marie asked me open-ended questions about myself, something I had not noticed her ever doing before. She smiled, but did not laugh with hilarity as she had a tendency to do before. She is doing a superior job and the managing partner for the firm is totally delighted. In several years it wouldn't surprise me is she was offered the job as managing partner.

INTELLECTUAL EXECUTIVES

Intellectual executives are more uncomfortable with feelings. They concentrate on what they think, not what they feel. They often come from finance or accounting, where they were trained in objectivity and quantitative analysis. Often they make it to the executive suite due to their financial expertise, their constant focus on the bottom line, their intellectual prowess, and their ability to make decisions.

Intellectual executives, by and large, have a high degree of willpower. This is where the intellectual executive has an edge. Trudging isn't a flashy activity, but when a career spans 40 years or so, an effective trudger is a long-term winner. Two other very useful traits underlie the intellectual's willpower. The first is concentration—the ability to tune out extraneous stimuli to focus on the important agenda. The intellectual also has organizational abilities and is able to prioritize objectives. This organization is necessary in order to focus optimal attention on the most worthwhile endeavors.

The intellectual can lack charisma and has a hard time motivating employees. Intellectual types often come into the leadership role after the business is up and running but needs better discipline and control. The structure exists; their function is to implement systems.

Intellectual executives tend to be more narrow-minded and they lack spontaneity. They have a hard time shooting from the hip and overcoming objections in a sales presentation. Their selling style is stable, monotone, and predictable. Most of the time, the company finds reasons to exclude them from presentations.

Intellectual executives supply, manipulate, and assemble data, but have trouble putting it all together when it comes to getting others to buy into the plan. These executives need to learn sales skills and to connect with themselves internally. They need to recognize their own emotions, and to be able visually and verbally to demonstrate excitement.

Intellectuals often look at sales training as a cost, not an investment. They question its value, and want demonstrable, bottom-line results from it. Sales training often doesn't have a bottom line; it's based on perceptions hard to measure. Intellectual executives *love* measurement. Intellectual executives like to focus on results, the final outcome.

Intellectual types, like in-house corporate accountants, usually consider sales necessary, but beneath them. They don't truly realize that sales are the heart and soul of a business. They must draw connections from their work to this heart and soul. The accounting department is the brain of an operation, but it doesn't drive it. Accounting is a historical science. To become better managers, intellectual executives must become achievement-oriented and concerned with activities that lead to profit, not the bottom line. Anybody can say no to ideas and trim budgets by eliminating expenditures. Intellectual executives must learn to contribute to the top line or gross of the business.

There are plenty of accountants on board full of ideas on improving the bottom line. Running a business by the numbers doesn't work. For short-term cost cutting, it may make sense, but for long-term strategies, it's foolish. Many leveraged buyouts in the 1980s were accomplished by having the finance people do it by the numbers. There was little appreciation or thought of keeping people informed, motivated, and excited. The results of these leveraged buyouts, in many cases, speak for themselves. They were colossal failures.

Training and development are investments, not costs. The intellectual executive must develop the ability to see the big picture and understand value systems and philosophies. I once conducted a strategic planning session for a company. After working with the vice president of human resources to set up the conference I asked to see the mission statement of the firm. A mission statement is the corporation's statement of what it feels destined to accomplish—the chosen end of their finest efforts. I was told that one did not exist. I said that this was an excellent place to begin the conference. Later, at the conference, I announced the agenda and gave a short speech on the purpose of a mission statement. The president, an engineer by training, cut me off. He said "I know you mean well, Dr. Watts. But we know what we do and how to do it here. Let's go to the next section." A mission statement is critical because it clearly states the ideals for which the corporation stands. People's emotions and perceptions of the company's ideals must be fostered and developed. Set ideals, then ask for ideas about reaching those goals.

Intellectual executives should go out on sales calls and get involved in understanding and measuring client needs. They should push back from their computers and take action. They should develop a sense of humor and not take themselves and their ideas so seriously.

By nature, intellectual executives are inherently critical hardheads. They must work to overcome this tendency to be critical and judgmental. Intellectuals tend to ignore their feelings and usually don't know themselves very well. They are trapped at the knowledge level, and don't transform knowledge into wisdom through the knowing of self.

Intellectuals are sometimes not good people-persons, and they usually don't realize this. They think they deal adequately, if not well, with people. After talking with many of their subordinates, I can say that, by and large, their people consider them standoffish, incommunicative, and uninspiring.

I would go so far as to say that any executive who shies away from sales is a poor executive. Many intellectual executives have told me "I'm not the kind of person who would do well at sales." There is no real self-examination of the issues that underlie a good executive salesperson. The intellectual has an oversensitivity: the fear of hearing "no." Repressed, they have lower self-esteem. The intellectual must learn to overcome the fear of rejection.

Because of sensitivity, early life was painful for the typical intellectual executive. Such executives use their intellect to avoid situations that might threaten their vulnerable self-esteem. They had a hard time getting a date to the junior prom. Their hands got cold and clammy when they had to talk to the opposite sex. More probably known as a "brain" in high school, they majored in a quantitative area in college. At parties, they tended to hang back and not introduce themselves—watch the action, so to speak.

The best therapy for intellectual executives is to get out of their comfort zone and cold-call an account. This is the easiest way to spot an intellectual executive—most won't even consider doing it. But if they'll just go with a salesperson on a call, their eyes will open. They'll begin to realize that their understanding of business was not as extensive as they thought. Slightly humbled, they're hopefully intrigued about increasing sales skills. An intellectual executive who takes sales courses, learns to cold-call, and promotes the company's business becomes a much finer executive—and rises to the top.

When intellectuals who haven't learned this balance get to the presidential suite and sales fall, they are at a loss. No matter how many formulas are put through the computer, the reality of the situation is that there aren't enough sales. The intellectual executive orders more and more sales reports, which are no help at all. When the intellectual executives see that sales are down, they need to focus their energy toward fostering optimism and working with the sales managers. They need to become active in sales by visiting customers, focusing on their market. The president must drive sales, regardless of whether she is an intellectual or an emotional executive. She can't worry or complain about a lack of sales; it's her responsibility to see that the gross of the business is there.

Tommy Schultz

Tommy Schultz is a 46-year-old gentleman who was sent to me for assessment after he had been fired from his company for not running his division effectively. The reasons for his dismissal were low productivity and an overall inability to manage. The president told me, "We stayed with Tom as best we could, but we just felt the division could be producing a profit, instead of barely breaking even for the past several years."

When I tested Tommy, he had an above-average intellectual ability—in the 95th percentile. Certainly he was smart enough for the job. He fell in the 20th percentile in terms of his extroversion. During our interview, I noticed he was detached, reserved, and impersonal. He didn't want to get close to me emotionally. People considered him shy.

However, he scored very high in dominance. He was aggressive, assertive, and competitive. Because of his intellectual ability, he felt superior. He was extremely sensitive to criticism, and had learned to tune out information critical of him. Remember, people who are sensitive to criticism are also susceptible to flattery, and Tommy craved the approval of others.

He had the tough-minded, no-nonsense approach to life that so many operational people have. I felt he was sincere, and sincerity can help an introvert be accepted in an extrovert's world. He had the ability to handle stress. His introversion, emotional detachment, and aloofness tended to distance the people below him. He never spent time with his employees off the job. When the workday was over, it was over; he retreated to his woodworking shop.

In a sense, Tommy only pretended to like people. On a deeper level, he was irritated by them. Intuitive people spotted this. They also picked up the fact that he thought he was superior intellectually. All of these things contributed to a slow deterioration of morale within his organization. He spent very little time with the salespeople or on the sales effort. Tommy liked to sit in his office reading operational reports.

Tommy wasn't a bad guy, but probably should have stayed in an administrative or accounting position where he didn't need true leadership skills. My recommendation for Tom was to go back to being a chief financial officer, or take another quantitative position. Unless he was willing to get out of his woodworking shop and go to sales training classes, there was no hope of his succeeding in the executive suite.

Robert Maruet

Robert Maruet, at the time I profiled him, was an executive whose position had just been eliminated; business was tight, and the company felt they could do without a vice president of administration. They sent Robert to me for some outplacement assessment services. They wanted me to help Robert understand what vocational pursuit he was best suited for.

Intellectual testing revealed that Robert's intelligence was in the 75th percentile. He had the ability to think quickly. He had a good value system, and honestly cared about people. He was diplomatic, and calculated his every move. As an administrator, he was very good at saying the right thing at the right time.

He was a serious person. His emotions were very restrained. Although he always said the right thing, you could tell that he didn't feel comfortable with people. He was threat-sensitive and hesitant to approach others. His underlying problem was a great amount of pride. He couldn't live up to his own high standards and was usually mildly depressed. He liked to keep a psychological distance from others and had a low need to get close to people. He wasn't very sociable and chose not to get to know his superiors on a personal level. He was conscientious and a hard worker, certainly self-disciplined, and had the ability to bear down, work hard, and get achievable results.

He was good enough at his job that during a decent economic period, he wouldn't have been fired. He certainly was no star, but there is a place for steady intellectuals in most companies. When the economy goes downhill, and it does from time to time, senior management looks for ways they can survive and retrench. They tend to cut the Robert Maruets from the corporate payroll, especially when they're paying them $150,000 a year.

One of the main reasons they decided to eliminate Robert was his inability to get close to his employees or bosses. His job was to see that the internal workings of the company were effective, and he did a decent job, but he didn't sell himself well within the organization. People around him felt he was competent, but they didn't particularly care for him or like him. There were no ill feelings, but there was no support for him, either. I feel that despite the tough economic times, if he'd established relationships with the senior executives in the company and understood what it took to fulfill their perception of his role, he wouldn't have been fired. He needed to become more enthusiastic on an interpersonal level. He also needed to overcome his sense of pride. He always shied away from any role where there was a chance he might fail. He needed to be more vocal—not aggressive, but to let people know where he stood.

Again, interpersonal selling skills would have been a tremendous help to him. I suggested this to him at the exit interview. He told me that he wasn't a salesperson, and that those skills are only needed for people who don't possess intellectual abilities. Perhaps so, Robert, but a little fluff is needed and wanted in America, and you'd better learn that or settle for a less-than-spectacular future.

Beth Allerton

Beth Allerton was the comptroller of a large manufacturing company. She was profiled to assess her strengths and weaknesses for the vice president of finance position. She was making a good salary and this promotion would pay almost double her current salary plus a bonus—a significant jump for Beth. The position was considered senior management and Beth would report directly to the president. The president liked Beth but felt she was a "numbers" person who did a good job as a top accountant but lacked the stature and interpersonal skills to make presentations to the board of directors and important customer prospects. I evaluated Beth and was impressed. I saw a person who had more interpersonal skills than what the president had suggested. What was really going on here? Why didn't Beth exhibit those skills more clearly?

Testing showed her to have an average or moderate need for people. She was bright, falling in the 85th percentile in intellect. She had passed her CPA exam, which has five parts, all in one sitting. She is the type who likes to plan ahead, does not like to take risks, and likes to be sure before she commits.

Obviously she was comfortable with numbers. This trait is associated with finance people, so there was nothing unusual here. She had a sincerity, a sense of quietness. I got the impression of a person who respected all humans equally. She made good eye contact and had a presence that created confidence with what she was telling you. Beth was 37 years old, and the president was 65. Beth revealed to me in her interview that the president intimidated her. Upon further questioning she revealed, reluctantly and with embarrassment, that she was an abused child and felt intimidated by older men. Her predicament became all too clear to me. She had to gain insight into the fact that subconsciously she equated the president with her father and knew from experience to "keep her mouth shut."

There are a lot of reports and testimonials coming out these days about how people were abused as children. This is fortunate because it helps people to understand themselves by seeing how others have worked through this type of trauma. It took some guts for Beth to sit down with the president and talk this issue over with him. The president was very sympathetic. They had an incredible talk that lasted 2½ hours. Both were exhausted, but reported that they felt close and believed they would not have any problems communicating in the future—and they haven't.

Beth got the job and is making a real contribution. They have formed a strong team with a great deal of mutual respect. Yes, she needs to work on her verbal presentation skills. She needs to be more comfortable in front of a group. She is gaining ground every day through training and mentoring from the president. I think that within five years Beth will be not only technically competent, but have the great interpersonal skills you can only develop when you accept yourself as a person and want genuinely to help others achieve competence in their lives as well.

FUSING THE TWO STYLES

The evolved, knowing executive is one who has fused his head and heart into a balanced whole. This makes an objective but emotionally sensitive person. There is no one way to perceive reality; both are valid. The rational, quantitative approach and the verbal, intuitive approach are both useful. Neither way is correct. No matter how we view the world, we are only partially correct. Some of what we believe is false.

Through fusion of the two main styles, we recognize that opinions are subjective, that our version of the truth is flawed, and that we filter truth through our emotions. We do so, and others do so. The best we can do is to try to look at the world as objectively as possible. Evolved executives don't squelch good ideas by demanding facts, nor do they buy into new ideas by being emotionally swayed. With evolved maturity, both types of executives can learn to grow. The intellectual types can learn to be more socially skilled, socially bold, and to believe in the power of passion. The emotional types can learn to concentrate and become more analytical. Fusion is the middle ground where a kind heart is kept in place by a wise head. Superior executives arise by balancing objectivity and emotionalism. Strive to plan and delay action if you're an emotional type, and use the converse if you're an intellectual type.

The two major types of executives are the way they are through a combination of genetics and their environment which shapes their thought process. They have defined themselves to themselves in a certain way. Both must destroy these assumptions, and redefine who they want to be and where they need to grow. They need to change their perceptions of themselves.

You need the objectivity of the intellectual side to make good decisions and the people skills of the emotional side to get others to buy into your decisions. When you fuse both styles, you develop characteristics from each management style. You have the two crucial points of being a successful executive: willpower and caring. These traits too rarely occur together. If you learn to persist in the face of obstacles *and* develop good relationships along your journey, your success is assured.

POWER LEADERSHIP TIPS

1. The need to dominate stems from unconscious fear. It is a powerful drive.
2. Don't interfere with your people's work—give guided freedom.
3. Pride produces separatism from your people.
4. Be a trainer in the spirit of cooperative goodwill.
5. Know your style, head or heart. Each has its inherent strengths and weaknesses.
6. Your goal is to fuse your head and heart into a balanced whole.

Chapter 5
Power Teams

THE CORPORATE TEAM MODEL

A team, group, or organization is an aggregate of human energies organized and arranged in a form that expresses the vision of the top executive. A useful model of a team is to think of people as electrons around the positive nucleus of an atom, which is the vision or goal of the group. This arrangement is the building block of life and teams. Teams are a constellation of energies, and the center of the energy is the executive.

Inner energy has been referred to as psychological cohesiveness, or team spirit. This is considered crucial for the team to produce at its optimal level. The team leader unfolds this higher group consciousness and leads the team to their greatest productivity. Good leaders create a sense of excitement, urgency, and inspiration. They instill optimism and enthusiasm.

As an executive, you are the magnetic center at the heart of your group. Your energy is what keeps the other energies together and moving forward. The power of your magnetism is dependent upon your ability to create a vision and motivate people to use their unique efforts and talents to make that vision a reality. As a top executive, this creation of group cohesiveness is one of your primary job responsibilities.

The conductor is the guiding energy of an orchestra. When an orchestra is well trained, and the conductor walks away, the orchestra plays on as if his energy were still there. In the long run, of course, the orchestra needs the conductor, as the team needs the executive. The executive ensures that the group's activity and energy are allied and focused. Team members supplement and reinforce each others' efforts and skills.

Your ability to develop positive team energy affects *your* energy. If, for example, you create a bad set of dynamics, making teamwork difficult, you will spend your energy dealing with personnel issues. You become the victim—or the beneficiary—of the energies you set into motion.

Executives must constantly remain aware of the status of their team's energy. One of the services my consulting firm provides is conducting "climate" or attitude and opinion surveys. The successful, dynamic executives are able to predict accurately the results of these surveys before they're tallied; they don't need the survey to give them feedback about how the employees view the company. Their sensitivity toward their team ensures that they can predict the results long before we enter them into the computer.

Cohesive teams make for enjoyable places to work. Cohesive team members value the group more highly and will defend it against internal and external threats. If they hear something negative about the company in their off-hours, they will be more likely to defend and promote the company instead of remaining silent or agreeing with the negative remarks. They will defend group standards and norms. Others within the organization will begin to conform to the team's levels of expected performance. When a new member is brought on board, the members will let her know subtly—or sometimes not so subtly—what behavior and values are expected.

One of our top salespeople was transferred from a rural office to our prime downtown location. The next time I saw her, she had a more stylish haircut, a beautifully tailored suit, and was driving a new luxury car. When I asked about the changes, she told me that after a few lunches and meetings with the team, she got the impression that if she was going to fit in, she would have to be "in style" with the rest of the group. Members of a cohesive team want to be accepted and approved of by the others. They accept and respect each other. This results in a willingness to give and receive help and be participatory—traits that are of immense value to you as leader.

A COMPANY'S TRUE VALUE

When a company is sold, the new owners buy the assets, the buildings, the inventory, *and* the group consciousness. New owners are typically much more concerned about the cash flow than the group consciousness. Business deals have a decidedly quantitative approach; cold, hard numbers are behind big decisions. Rarely does someone put money into a deal because of attitudes, or even bother trying to determine what they are. A new owner's primary interest is to improve the bottom line; after all, interest must be paid on all borrowed money! A quick way to do this is to cut the biggest expenditure: the number of employees. This is called "cutting the fat out."

But they're not cutting fat, they're cutting people, and morale takes a nosedive. Decreased productivity is the inevitable result. Deals which looked so financially attractive on paper turn south after the acquisition. The quality that attracted the new owners to the company is defused. Cash flow is an outer manifestation of the group's inner consciousness. Cash flow is a quantifiable measure of group synergy. Once defused, group consciousness and synergy can be redeveloped, but it's harder the second time around because of an understandable lack of trust. The perception among the rank and file is that the new owners are out strictly for a bottom-line improvement. Employees become reluctant to give of themselves; they only give agreed-upon time. The new owners want hard work, but it's hard to be dedicated and loyal when you're considered "fat." It doesn't take a management consultant long to discover what everybody else knows: the employees don't like or respect the new owners. The word processors turn out lots of resumes during the lunch hour and after 5:30.

The true value of a company is in the quality and amount of its group consciousness. Group consciousness is hard to develop. It's difficult to recruit, train, and develop employees. The perception is that it is easier to buy a company than create one from scratch. When parent companies take the path of least resistance and buy a "turnkey" company, however, it often turns out to be a disappointment. Companies often want to buy other companies because they don't have the recruiting ability, energy, or mental stamina to build one. Like the individual who takes the path of least resistance, a company can take the path of least resistance—with the same predictably bad results.

Many companies don't want to put money into training and development; they want to go out and hire experienced and capable people. This seems to be especially true when building a sales team. At first glance, this makes for good reading. It's nice to think that a company could eliminate training overhead by hiring experienced professionals.

Unfortunately, by taking the path of least resistance and not putting money into training and development, companies never create the consciousness they need. Morale problems and turnover result. The president of a startup company asked me to help him build a sales team. We met, and I told him how I would go about it. First, I'd develop a job description and analysis to get a firm idea of what the salespeople would have to do to be successful. Next, I'd recruit aggressively the most qualified people I could pay. When I had my team, I'd put them through an orientation and training program which serves two very important purposes: developing success habits and forming a company culture.

He disagreed. He told me that since this was a startup company but not a startup industry, his solution was to simply "headhunt"—steal his competitors' people. I'd seen this strategy tried unsuccessfully in several other businesses, and I related these experiences to him. He maintained that in his case it would work; he was willing to offer higher commissions, a better deal. He intended to make very enticing offers to proven producers who were primarily interested in money. He said, smiling, "Salespeople's number one desire is a higher commission split."

After a year and a half of nearly 200 percent turnover from the "stars" the president recruited, he called to invite me to work with his company to set up a more professional recruiting program combined with a solid training program. He admitted that the people he recruited were *only* interested in money. His competition played the same game he played to entice the best people—with diminishing returns for all involved. He told me his stars were selfish, next to impossible to deal with, and had no commitment to the company, only to themselves.

Some salespeople do think of money as their number-one goal, and it's true that they're usually rotten team players. They cause a lot of divisiveness internally. They tend to argue over commission checks and, true to their philosophy, they complain that they're undercompensated—you can imagine the effects of *that* team dynamic. These people aren't bad human beings; they simply should form their own private enterprises. Both they and the companies they serve would come out ahead.

Group consciousness is as real as the building and furniture that house it—and certainly of more value. A company that's built on the basis of financial transactions or headhunting is never as solid as the one built by selecting employees one by one and then shaping, building, and training each one to be a proud member of the team.

SPECIFIC ROLES AND ATTRIBUTES OF THE TEAM LEADER

Modeling

The executive is the focal point for the team. People look to the team leader for answers and behavioral cues to help them decide what they need to do in order to be successful within the company. This focus of attention provides an excellent opportunity for the skilled motivator to model a value system for the company, but this opportunity is frequently missed.

I recently evaluated a superstar salesperson who desperately wants to be made head of the branch office. She feels she deserves it. After all, she has been the company's top producer for three years. She's 50 years old and wants to "go somewhere in her career." Unfortunately, only six months ago she became angry with the office manager and with one hand cleared off the top of a desk, shattering a vase and scattering papers, reports, and wet broken glass over half the office. During our session when she related this incident to me, she said confidently, "I don't think it'll hurt my chances. I can motivate people and train them to be top-flight salespeople—and management knows it."

She does have these abilities. But she overlooked the possibility that her superiors may not want her team to model on that type of behavior. An executive should be a model of maturity for the group to emulate. This incident made it difficult for the other team members to look to her to help them put things into perspective. In fact, in *their* sessions they revealed to me that they were very much bothered by her lack of control. She found out soon after just how bothered they really were; she didn't get the job, and quit shortly thereafter.

If you'll take some time to listen to a team, you'll be struck by the number of conversations devoted to discussing, evaluating, and analyzing the leader's behavior. Leaders are influential individuals. You can't afford to be a thrower or a screamer in today's business world.

As an executive, you are in charge of translating the corporation's vision and goals for your division and each employee in it. It's vital for each member to understand both the team's goal and his individual goals—your cohesiveness depends on it. Unity of goals leads to team harmony. Each member of your team can only apply his personality and aptitudes if he has a clear vision of where he's going. He must understand the obstacles that will be faced. The motive for his actions should be pure and simple in his mind.

Executives must see themselves as trainers who teach group members to focus on the corporate vision. Teach them to visualize the company's role in business and their individual role within the company. When training, communicate your reasoning, then give the instructions and demonstration necessary to develop the habits, thoughts, and behavior of excellence. If your people don't understand the expected form and their role in creating it, they can't be expected to make good decisions. These goals, when they're clearly understood, serve as an ideal reference point. The ideal is the best the team can be if it uses its energy and commitment. All decisions emanate from this point.

As team leader, work to establish and develop corporate virtues, ideals of the team's maximum effort combined with a morally fit goal. For example, the most important virtue for the human resource department is commitment to recruit, hire, and train the finest employees in the industry. The virtue for the marketing department might be to promote the products with ethical aggression, achieving the highest sales in the industry. The group's direction is determined by the quality of these virtues. Analyze your department. Look for the virtues you are responsible for, and cultivate your team's understanding of these virtues and help it aim for them.

One president I know wanted to emphasize that the company was going to go national and that there would be no stopping the momentum; it was going to "take off." For the meeting in which he introduced the company's vision and marketing plan, he made up the long hallway in the corporate office to look like the inside of a plane. The top executives were the flight attendants. They created an in-house "movie" for the "flight." Through demonstration and analogy, he reinforced his vision and got people fired up. Nobody wanted to parachute from this corporate plane. People were on board!

Teaching—and Living—Ego Restraint

In order to reach the ideal the group is capable of, which benefits all, each member must sacrifice some personal desires or ego for group achievement. It's especially important that you, as the leader, demonstrate your willingness to sacrifice in a meaningful way too. Treat yourself as well as your team, and no better. Executive dining rooms and executive parking facilities are divisive; they exist only to appease the egos of the executives.

A company president once complained to me that the parking lot did not have enough parking spaces close by. He announced he was going to reserve the 10 best spaces for himself and the nine vice presidents. I pointed out that—theoretically—this wasn't necessary; if the top executive team were, as they claimed, the hardest-working group in the company, they ought to get to work early enough to get the best parking spaces. He thought it over for a day, and decided I was right. To this day, his company's rule is "first come, first parked!"

Here's a useful way to evaluate teams. An executive's maturity level is the barometer of the team's maturity. The team's stability is a reflection of the executive's emotional stability. The executive's personality must be subordinate to the collective consciousness of the group. Executives must keep their humility and sense of proportion. Keep your ego separated from the team goal, and realize that it is the *group* striving toward the goal that is the important issue.

In my experience, I find that most executives—including myself—tend to overestimate their leadership ability and contributions. They feel their team's success is in large part due to their contributions, insight, and energy. They don't realize that they're being carried forward by the tide of other people's efforts. Quite commonly in my consulting work, executives ascribe great importance to themselves and to their leadership ability. I have learned that a far more accurate measure of an executive's ability is the group's evaluation of the leader's contribution.

Bear this simple thought in mind: you yourself are relatively unimportant, but the mass of the group has tremendous potency. Collectively, a group has much more insight, has more perspective, is more multifaceted, and can develop many more solutions than any of you ever could singly. You personally don't count for much, but the collective consciousness of the group *does* count.

I have seen many examples in the business world of executives who overestimate their talents and abilities. They get angry at their company for not listening to them and decide to leave and start their own companies. When they go belly-up—broke—it's because they don't have the capacity they thought they did. It's very interesting to talk with these "successful" corporate executives turned "failed" entrepreneurs. Their justifications for their failures are certainly creative! I'm not suggesting that some who read this book shouldn't quit their jobs and start their own companies; they probably will be very successful and would be doing themselves a real disservice by not going the entrepreneurial route. Again, view yourself realistically and objectively—not through rose-tinted lenses. Don't allow your ego to become too big when you are appointed an executive. Be humble and realize that your role is to energize the team. The team's energy is quite powerful—

more powerful than yours could ever be. Turn away from personal issues to the larger issues of the group.

It's also important to realize that your people, taken as a whole, are probably not inherently much better than your competitor's people. Any statistician or industrial psychologist will point out that, mathematically, people don't deviate too far from the average. About 70 percent of us fall within the average range. Overall individual ability doesn't vary much from corporation to corporation, but management's ability to fuse their energies does. Doing this well is the most important contribution you can make.

Demonstrate teamwork by speaking well of other departments within your organization, and manifesting the spirit of goodwill in settling problems. The level of cohesiveness in a company is affected and impacted by race, nationality, heredity influences, the environment, and the diversity of life experiences. Quality teams do their best to eliminate prejudices and personal pride. These two factors destroy the fabric of team spirit. Quality teams have as few internal secrets as possible. As a team leader, be quite careful about having secrets with a certain section of your department or with individuals. Secrets are destructive, and they diminish your stature. There is a difference between being confidential and having secrets. Being confidential implies intimacy and trust; being secretive implies privilege, concealment, or clandestineness. An "us versus them" mentality within your team carries the virus of low productivity and low company morale.

People who operate with a lower level of maturity need "enemies." As a team matures, the members will need fewer outside enemies in order to focus and direct their energy, or to define themselves. I was once in charge of a corporate strategic planning retreat. My role was to coordinate the various thoughts from the group members and get the group to operate as proficiently as possible. The senior vice president of marketing gave a presentation on what the company was going to do to meet the sales goals for the year. The gist of his speech was "How to defeat the enemy"—our competitors. The president, an extremely successful and happy man whom I greatly admire, told the meeting participants, "It's important to the company to be successful, but our competition is not the enemy. We don't need to throw slings and arrows at our competitors to help us define ourselves. The real enemy is a lack of synthesis, the stifling of creativity, and separateness. I'm more interested in understanding our weaknesses, not our competitors' weaknesses." He always spoke well of the competition and showed respect for the industry he was in. His integrity and his own considerable success ensures that his industry will always respect *him*.

OVERCOMING FEAR

One of your primary executive roles is to help your team members overcome fear. Until their fears are overcome, their innate goodness can't be manifested. What are they afraid of? Team members fear not being recognized as competent. They fear they won't understand what's going on. They fear their voices won't be heard. They fear they'll be fired. When fears present themselves, team morale goes into a slump. Attitudes become progressively worse. This is especially true when top management is viewed with suspicion.

History offers us countless examples of wonderful, positive group consciousness and teamwork, and other examples of negative group consciousness. Negative group consciousness features survival instincts as the core energy. As is true in the individual, groups needs to overcome the grip of the survival instinct. Lower-order tendencies must be subordinated to the higher-order tendencies of teamwork and selflessness. When the executive creates the feeling of excitement and the future looks promising, members' survival instincts move to the background.

One of my favorite client presidents, Herbert Carrel, is a gifted team leader. When the savings and loan industry collapsed in the early 1990s, his company's parent institution, a troubled savings and loan, was taken over by the government in the form of the Resolution Trust Corporation. The RTC's plan was to sell off assets, find buyers for the companies, and then sell them to the highest bidder to reduce the losses the government suffered through the failed savings and loans.

Herb was ready when the RTC came through his door. He showed courage and leadership. He urged all of his executives to stay with him, to believe they'd find the right buyer, and to out-hustle the competition. He reassured them they'd all come out of the situation with their jobs, their security, and their careers intact. Although the sale took almost two years, not one valuable executive left the company, and his vision was finally manifested. Through the power of his belief and his focus on the vision—not the *impediments* to the vision—he negated the fears of his people. He got them to focus on the goal, not the day-to-day disappointments, and he and his team were rewarded. The still-intact group is thriving under the new ownership. Herb's standing among the executives vaulted to an even higher level.

DEALING WITH CONFLICT

Conflict is the result of colliding viewpoints and opposing loyalties. When people interact and wrestle with differing points of view, truth emerges. The executive must show that the needs of the group are meaningful enough to bear the discomfort of working through interpersonal difficulties and differing strategies to be successful. Be aware of separate energies, but don't recognize them or focus on them. Dissension is of relatively minor importance, all things considered. Don't ignore it, but don't allow it to be a distraction. As the team leader, project the attitude of desiring to push the group's energies ahead. Show that you don't have time for trifles and nonessentials. Hold the goal—not the conflict—in front of the group. Conflict is the pathway towards unity. Coming to grips with, working through, and resolving conflict cements a team.

It is also one of the best opportunities for you to demonstrate leadership and set an example. This means that, as the team leader, you must allow members of the group to disagree openly with you, too. You'll lose valuable members of your team and the rest of the group's esteem if you don't.

Executives realize that without a certain amount of "storming," a group can't perform. *Storming* is the struggle in which each person's position, role, and specific strategy gets defined. This conflict brings development, and it is inevitable; in fact, its absence signifies a lack of creativity.

There are as many ways for conflict to develop as there are people. Rivalry develops between managers competing for a newly created position. They may vie for the largest share of the executive's attention, to be the most powerful, or to get the most noticed and rewarded assignments. Team members will try to accumulate power—this is not preventable. The leader helps people clarify and understand the real issues causing the conflict. Storming is ongoing, and will continuously recur despite successful resolution of past conflicts. The team leader can't allow constant storming to be the norm, but must realize that conflict is necessary in order for the team members to understand their roles.

Team players do break down into various roles. Some of your team players will be leaders—one may even be your replacement. Others will be good lieutenants and followers. One member may emerge whose role is to reduce interpersonal tension, when it gets dangerously high, through the use of humor. Another team member may be responsible for providing encouragement when activities begin to drag. Someone else with a tendency to nurture may provide recognition to those who work especially hard.

Team leaders introduce and guide conflict positively by the skillful use of guided questioning. They help group members express anger directly and fairly. Help team members who are unable to express their anger to take risks and learn that such behavior is okay. Team members must feel secure that you won't allow information to be taken out of context. They must know that information that was given under conditions of trust won't be used against them later. In the ideal group setting, communication is open, viewpoints are flexible, and a non-possessive warmth pervades. People feel free in expressing their opinions.

The executive must focus the team's energy by helping its members control their emotions. Put another way, the executive's role is to socially synthesize the group and provide peace. Correct communication and human relations are at the heart of team spirit. Executives provide peace by being at peace with themselves. An executive rarely displays negative emotions publicly, unless it's done for a specific effect. Negative emotions are rarely inspirational or motivating. They only salve the executive's ego.

Organizational peace is a proactive willingness to confront situations that need to be resolved; it is not inert pacifism, but rather an active goal. Cohesiveness does not imply psychological comfort. Unless conflict is openly expressed, attitudes develop which hamper effective performance. Unexpressed hostility simply smolders and seeps out in many indirect, sometime passive ways, none of which enhance the group's creativity.

It isn't easy to communicate honestly with someone you dislike, and the team leader will occasionally have to harmonize two people who don't like each other. The leader realizes that adversaries must continue to work together in a meaningful way and be willing to go beyond name calling so they can get down to productive work. People with a great deal of antagonism toward each other have the potential to be of the greatest value to each to other. Obviously they care about what the other thinks—otherwise they wouldn't be so angry! If you really don't care about who or what another person is, or have little respect for him, you don't *get* angry; you're indifferent. By demonstrating correct communication behavior and controlling emotions, the team leader gets the two disgruntled members to express their thoughts openly.

Leaders must be able to deal with their own nervousness and anxiety and not be afraid of that nasty feeling in the pit of their stomach. To succeed at peacemaking, you must be able to wait out prolonged periods of silence where all three of the participants feel psychologically uncomfortable. Work on being able to restate problems without being accusatory.

Leaders must be willing to take communication and emotional risks, if need be, to demonstrate how they expect the other team members to interact. This can be done by occasionally pointing out faults and flaws in their own thinking. Group leaders can do a great deal to forward communication if they will self-disclose some of the emotions they are experiencing. Don't show great weakness, whine, feel sorry for yourself, or project that the problems are too difficult for the team; too much self-disclosure is negative. The leader must stand apart from the team psychologically and be seen as a source of strength and inspiration. *Selectively* reveal your feelings. Obviously, don't share with your team the fact that you think a fellow executive is mediocre or too aggressive. A good executive is never publicly defamatory, nor does she talk about her fears to any great extent. Be able to honestly, tactfully share how you feel and perceive an issue—it does much to establish you as the leader and as the model of maturity for the team.

If leaders fail to disclose how they truly feel, they don't get valid feedback from the group, and the team represses conflict. Honest self-disclosure has long been correlated with a high level of self-esteem. People who don't self-disclose are usually very controlled, and controlled executives do little to get their group fired up and motivated. Encourage openness and directness. Reiterate to the group that no one has any right to attack someone personally, but that ideas for the company are open for discussion.

One of the major reasons why teams don't form and become cohesive is because the members don't explicitly discuss the ongoing process of the group interaction. In other words, they don't tell each other when they disagree with what's happening. They aren't honest with each other in describing how they feel about what the other team member is doing or saying. This leads to a lack of trust; people begin to view their own actions as honest and straightforward and those of the other members of the team as scheming, unreasonable, and backstabbing. As the group leader, you must be able to process the dynamics of the group while they're happening. The group executive has to ask the questions that create the dynamics of team members being able constructively to tell the truth to each other. People never believe that their opinions are distorted or wrong. All beliefs we hold seem true to us. In conflict, all parties believe their own ideas and methods are right and others' are wrong. Try to get people to rethink their steadfastness of opinion by getting them to restate the problem from the other's viewpoint.

Most of us have been involved in a group meeting conducted by an authoritarian. The head of the group meeting thinks she is offering an idea up for discussion, but in actuality she is seeking conformance to her point of view. The way she introduces the topic, her body language, her tone of voice, and so forth, alert the team that the only discussion wanted is that which agrees with her idea. The rest of the team looks like those wire-necked dolls in the backs of car windows, their heads are nodding up and down so fast! People aren't stupid; they're not going to give their opinion when it's going to negatively impact their future.

Cohesiveness also fails to occur when the group members don't really respect each other. Group members who don't respect each other's knowledge and skill usually just act as if they do. The team leader must deal with this directly and decisively. Dominating, egotistical people often lack respect for other members of the team, particularly when they consider themselves intellectually superior. Don't back down or be intimidated by the intellectually superior, dominant team member. If it takes a confronting situation in which you point out the faults and deficiencies of the aggressive team member, do so. It is your challenge to get the aggressive member to feel respect for the other members of the team by pointing out their virtues and contributions. The dominating intellectual member's contribution doesn't compensate for the subtle deterioration of the team's morale.

Many times, an intellectually superior member of a team uses this superiority to gain psychological advantage by intimidating the other members. His emotional maturity, the other half of the equation, is often woefully underdeveloped, almost to the point of being juvenile. These types do a great deal of subtle destruction, and in a group meeting stifle creativity and group processing. People censor their comments because they know they will be intellectually challenged. The dialogue doesn't run free and easy; it's controlled and stilted.

Presidents often refuse to fire these obnoxious individuals because they know so much about the business. Again, it is an intuitive judgment call as to whether to fire somebody or keep trying to counsel them about their behavior. One of my client companies reached an interesting solution to this problem. A particularly obnoxious but brilliant marketing executive was "fired" and then rehired as a consultant. Normally I wouldn't recommend this action. In this case, when this guy's power was stripped, and he had to sell his way back into the company and then sell his ideas, it made a huge difference in his behavior. No longer could he be brusque or demeaning, or else he would lose his contract—a darned good one, I might add. Their consulting relationship continues to this day, five years later. The person has done a real about-face; he has several more clients and is not a bad guy now!

Without mutual respect, there is also more splitting off of "subgroups." This occurs to some extent in any event. These factions, subunits of the larger team, develop when people feel they can get more done, or enjoy work more if they don't have the rest of the team to interfere with them. There is nothing wrong in team members going out to lunch with each other, but if this is taken too far and sniping and gossiping or status becomes an issue, the leader must step in and emphasize the whole group instead of just certain members of the group. Subgrouping can be partially alleviated by the team leader taking out different pairings of people to lunch or even having a group lunch on a quarterly basis.

Subgroups can often be subtly destructive to the team by always agreeing with each other, ganging up on other team members, and so forth. People who feel excluded lose team spirit and morale. They are typically very unwilling to discuss this problem; it's embarrassing, and sounds juvenile to tattle to the leader of being kept outside the clique. Team splintering reflects badly on the leadership of the executive. I have noticed team factions form readily under dictatorial leaders. As a team leader, don't encourage subgroups by your actions. When you play favorites, you set the dynamics to destroy the greater team cohesiveness.

FREEDOM

The more guided freedom people have, the stronger the infrastructure is. When guided freedom is lacking, bureaucracy threatens. Freedom needs to be a part of the corporate culture. Make the giving of freedom part of your team-building style. Executives develop unselfishness in their people and give them the power to do the right thing. Develop your team's ability to handle freedom through education and training. Applaud the individualistic value system on which our country was founded. Inherent in individualism lies group strength. An objective individual who decides to give herself emotionally to the group is a more deeply committed member of the group. When objective team members know, understand, and approve of the facts behind a situation and are still swayed by the power of the company's ideals, it is a powerful and synergistic team.

Employees' motivation increases with freedom. Authoritarian sales executives are frequently surprised at how sales go up when they're on vacation. Without them there, their people have freedom to do what they think is right. Their energy is focused on the endeavor, not on trying to impress the boss or conform to his wishes. Although the increase in sales is a delightful thing to return to, the executive feels it's only a statistical quirk, nothing else. It's not as much of a quirk as the executive likes to think! On a day-in, day-out, short-term basis, the team doesn't need as much of the executive's energy as the executive likes to think. Learn to detach yourself, and congratulate your people on being detached from you. This ultimately is what both parties want, and it frees up energy that can be devoted to more creative uses. Freedom leads to productivity. Be involved, but have enough emotional detachment to be objective.

Case Study: A Great Team Builder

Truly great team builders are rare in business. The best I've met is Tom Higgins, a senior vice president of human resources of a large motel company. Tom is a large man physically. A former Southwest Conference tight end, he has a delicate, totally coordinated walk which belies his six-foot-three, 235-pound frame. Tom has an exceptional intellect, in the 99th percentile. His personality, with its flaws, is the profile of a great team builder and coach-type executive. I have seen him ignore my recommendation not to hire somebody, and within a relatively short period of time turn a loser into a contributing team winner.

I have known Tom for over 10 years and have helped him hire 50 people. Amazingly, nobody has ever failed under Tom; every one has made personal and professional progress. Tom is one of the few human resource professionals I have seen who really should be president of a company, and I think his profile is the profile of a future president. Our future presidents are the type who are able to inspire and motivate people to make a commitment to excellence, which is what Tom is capable of. Tom has a high people need, falling within the 90th percentile. He is warm-hearted, very outgoing, and very group-oriented. He truly likes people. I don't think there is any substitute for this dimension in an effective team builder's personality.

You can be successful as an executive without being a super team builder and not having a real love for people, but I really don't think you can be a super team builder without this dimension. Tom likes to be included in group activities, but he is at his best leading a team. He is a dominating personality, but this is balanced by his high level of sensitivity, genuine honesty, and caring about his people. His measured sensitivity is also in the 90th percentile, which would make it difficult for him to be in sales because he would get his feelings hurt in a strictly cold-call situation. He is assertive, competitive, and can occasionally be close-minded when he thinks he's right (he will deny this!).

His real team-building and leadership skill is his intuitiveness—it borders on psychic ability. This is where his profile has a lot of "feminine energy." We are all a blend of both feminine and masculine energies. Dominating, angry executives—male or female—have not balanced their masculine energies with feminine energies. They need to awaken more nurturing and not be afraid of this dimension of their personalities. The overly passive "don't-kick-me-too-hard" types have not developed their masculine energies enough and are too soft and pliable as a result. On many occasions, Tom's people have told me that they were thinking of something, and he will call them into his office and propose a project that was exactly what they were thinking about! Tom is an amazingly creative guy. I have seem him give training retreat presentations to 500 people that were so interesting, unusual, and dynamic they would have made Steven Spielberg envious! There is always something happening: spontaneous skits or hired actors paid to play roles that reinforce his point.

In a meeting, he understands the inner and outer workings of a group. What is not being said is as loud and clear to him as to what is being said. He will draw out the silent or intimidated person, and make her the "star" of the meeting, which totally changes the way she perceives her life and role within the company. He is a fantastic public speaker, easily arousing the hardest-core finance person with his liveliness and energy.

Tom is mentally healthy. Unbeknownst to most of his staff, he has a very evolved and ongoing religious development program. I have found that executives who have a strong religious and spiritual basis make better team builders. These evolved belief systems are usually completely unobtrusive; not even their closest peers at work know anything about this sphere of their lives. This quality is most pronounced in Tom, and he was reluctant to share it with me because he feels that spirituality is an individual thing, not appropriate in the vast majority of settings, most certainly work. Tom grew up in a small Texas town where life was tough physically but rich spiritually. He reaches back to his foundations, both philosophical and early learning, for his guidance, and seems to make full use of his lifespan because of his great amount of personal introspection.

Tom doesn't like rules and regulations. He gives his people lots of latitude to try new things, and they are allowed to fail. He is a delegator. His people tell me behind his back that he expects the impossible, but he usually gets it! People simply work their butts off for Tom for a salary that is modest. Usually I wouldn't expect people to stay up till three in the morning, collapse on the rug of his office, and be at a 7:30 breakfast meeting the next day eager to pick up where they left off, but they'll do it for Tom. The difference is that Tom will have gotten there an hour early to make sure each of his people has a small present and a special handwritten thank-you note. One woman who has been with Tom for over 10 years has kept every one of his personal notes. She refers to them when she feels she needs inspiration or to renew her confidence.

REFLECTIONS OF YOUR FAMILY

Unconsciously, the manner by which you relate to your team stems from the kind of family structure and interaction with which you were raised. We are deeply conditioned by our families. We unconsciously manage others as we were managed by our parents. People rarely think through where their most important beliefs and value systems originate. They carry around a bunch of opinions about how to manage and motivate a team that they have not really thought through. We occasionally reflect back on our parents' idiosyncrasies and wonder how they could be objective about certain areas of their lives and so totally biased about other areas. Don't look now, but your children and employees are thinking the same thing about you!

The definition of a cohesive team, like that of an effective family, is the quality of esprit de corps. The goals of a family are simple and straightforward—to provide a sense of security, a sense of belonging, and the freedom to become individuals. The same definition and goals characterize a quality team. The definition of a poor team is one that lacks integration (cohesiveness) and ability to adapt to new stresses. A dysfunctional team is like a dysfunctional family—chaotic and impulsive. Dysfunctional families are constantly in emotional turmoil. Dysfunctional teams are noneffective. Functioning in a family, as a team, is mostly a nonverbal process—it's not so much what you say as how you act. It is the emotional intensity that causes problems, not the specific issues. Emotionality drives human relationships.

Two major forces are always in adjustment on any team or family. People want individuality and autonomy, but they also have an instinctual need for others and desire a sense of being connected. There can be too much togetherness; a family can be together too much. Neither fosters individual creativity and identity. But there must be some togetherness or it isn't a well-functioning family or team. When people become too close there will be an incident or a series of incidents that will cause the people to move towards individualization, correcting the balance.

Many families communicate in a "triangular" fashion. They don't speak directly to whom they desire, but speak to another person to communicate the message. Thus a triangle is created. Such a pattern of communicating is seen in the corporate world. Some executives want somebody on their team to change their behavior. Instead of an honest, tactfully direct conference, they tell somebody what is irritating them, figuring the remark will finds its way back to the person they should have discussed it with initially. But, because they lacked the confidence needed (i.e., they didn't feel they could handle the power of their uncomfortable emotions) they took a circuitous route of communication. This form of communication is considered unhealthy by family therapists and is just as unhealthy for an organization. In general, when two people distance themselves, one person, the more uncomfortable one, resolves the relationship dilemma by moving towards a third person. We see this pattern in families when a husband and wife don't get along and one spouse moves towards one of the children to form a closer relationship. In any human triangle, there are two insiders and one outsider. Executives re-create the same unhealthy pattern they grew up with in a business setting, oblivious to the antecedent conditioning which created their behavior. They create a series of people triangles with people rotating through the role of being out or in, depending on which triangle they are moving to or from. Thus, as in the dysfunctional family, there is an underlying lack of directness and clarity.

Another form of management behavior which stems from the family's style of upbringing is the authoritarian who demands conformance to black or white rules. Controlling parents who exhibit rigidity, extreme punishment, and emotional constriction foster the future controlling authoritarian in the workplace. Many families simply don't know how to play and have fun. A certain playfulness is needed for growth and creativity. When teams don't have fun together, don't expect them to produce anything more than what they have to to keep their jobs. When families don't have fun together, don't expect them to interact any more than is necessary to maintain peace. Executives raised in overly serious homes believe that having fun at work is not appropriate. Rigid, standoffish people like to communicate by memos and behavioral objectives. When people become polarized in their beliefs (as authoritarians do), they do so based on emotionality. The ability to tolerate differences and see differences as valuable is a characteristic of a more evolved team leader. It indicates a high level of differentiation of self and is usually the result of the parents respecting the child's opinions. Good parents, like good team builders, foster the attitude of having a very small percentage of correct answers. Evolved managers understand that it is best if they take the attitude of only having a reasonably accurate set of assumptions. This leads to an inquiring, contemplative attitude, rather than a fix-it-or-make-it-go-away attitude.

A paranoid family that is profoundly suspicious turns out future executives who are nitpicky, sneaky, and defensive. If you come from a family of lesser means, how did your parents react when they saw people with greater wealth? Was there a feeling of jealously and resentment? The executive raised in these circumstances insists that all answers come from him because he can't tolerate anybody being better.

Infantile delusion of grandeur, usually resulting from an overpraising mother, creates an executive who insists that people praise her. She is very amenable to being influenced by flattery and will favor people who tell her how wonderful she is. When parents focus too much on one of their children, the child can grow up too sensitive and selfish. They are more vulnerable to the development of mental, physical, or social problems.

Executives can play the role of a "white knight." Rescuing employees and helping them in any possible way, even to the point where they won't allow people to stand on their own two feet, seems natural to these knights. These so-called nice people are so preoccupied with doing good for others they become non-people in the process. They are not able to say, "This is who I am and this is what I believe." Acceptance by the group is more important than living by a deeply felt belief system. They won't risk rejection and possible isolation. People who unrealistically think that it is their responsibility to preserve harmony and a sense of emotional well-being in family relationships can be so opposed to conflict they repress real underlying issues.

Generally one person gives more in a marriage. This behavior can carry over to work. When one person gives in to the other based on *emotional factors,* as opposed to specific *expertise* or *objective data,* complications result. A similar pattern develops when one spouse focuses on pleasing the other. He will compromise his real viewpoint to gain approval and preserve harmony. He feels inadequate and doesn't see himself as capable of holding opinions or having thoughts of his own. The other spouse is seen as independent, cool, and unemotional—overvaluing herself and criticizing the seeming inadequacy of her spouse. Both people have a problem. Whichever parent the executive modeled himself after will have the same problem. He will either compromise himself by trying too hard to please others, or create (falsely) a sense of superiority based on the illusion of always being right. In some families one spouse sometimes feels she knows what is best for the other. She anxiously monitors the functioning of the other to keep him on track. This kind of anxious hovering can impair the other's ability to function. These people carry this same anxiousness into the world of work, where they refuse to delegate and hover over people to make sure they are doing the work right. The group can't move ahead any faster than the executive can supervise every minute detail. These managers also act as mentors to their younger staff members, who are conditioned to managing in a similar fashion. Thus, bureaucracies are created and perpetuated.

Conflict in a group, like in a family, takes several familiar themes. People can simply distance themselves so as not to arouse emotions. When as a child you observed tension between your mother and father, and it resulted in your parents simply not talking about it and one parent leaving, you will have a tendency to do the same thing—simply retreating to your office and pretending the difficulties aren't there. People can distance themselves by avoiding certain subjects. Some families have taboo topics which they avoid. Corporate teams are no different. People simply refuse to discuss certain agenda items because they know it will cause their superior to react emotionally. People won't speak to each other, or even look at each other for extended periods.

Emotional distancing *reflects* a problem (lack of mature communication skills), *solves* a problem (alleviates the anxiety of the moment), and *creates* a problem (distancing isolates and alienates people from each other). The anxiety, and the series of compromises people make to allay the anxiety, mount up over time. Tensions can be reduced by one person giving in to the other to maintain harmony. But compromises are usually short-term solutions that come back to haunt the system.

If parents who believe they aren't assertive see—even for a split second—their child being nonassertive, they single out that behavior. They reinforce it in their child by making a big deal out of it and blowing it out of proportion, thus projecting their feelings of inadequacy onto the child. Eventually, as an adult, the daughter will believe she has an assertiveness problem. As a result, she will not like to confront negative employees. Nobody wants to hurt another, not really. Everybody loses something in the process. I've never met parents who deliberately wanted to transfer their negative qualities on to their children; but we all do. Like a family, a work team can be impaired, but still function. Challenge yourself to understand how and where your belief systems come from. More times than not, we see our parents reflected in our behavior as their behavior reflects that of their parents.

Systems theory in family therapy conceptualizes that relationships between people cause the problems that a person has. A good therapist looks at the family as a whole and does not necessarily pick out one person and label her the "problem." Interestingly, industry is beginning to catch on to a systems approach for evaluating people. Instead of blaming the person for not living up to expectations as is usually the case in performance reviews, another way of looking at the problem is to look at the system, the entire environment, and ask, "What is it about our system of operating that does not bring out the best in this person?"

No person can be understood and motivated out of the context of his or her important relationships. No relationship can be understood out of the context of the way it interlocks with other relationships. Looking for the "cause" of behavior is usually senseless and unrewarding. It is like asking a person why he did something. There is a multitude of interdependent factors that cause any one behavior. Thinking about an individual as an isolated human being and thinking about him as part of a system are two entirely different ways of perceiving and conceptualizing human behavior. When a child is experiencing behavioral problems, it does little good to have him see a therapist. The therapist must look at the child as being a part of the whole which must be addressed. When an employee is having behavioral problems, you must look at him as a part of the whole team.

Reflecting on your family—the way your parents communicated, the way people acted at the dinner table, the way your parents broke bad news, the way you were treated by your siblings—can be revealing. Deep within your mind lie the remnants of these interactions. Although you may not be able to recall many of the specifics, the patterns were created. It is a point of growth to recognize these patterns and deduce how they affect the ways you relate to your team.

TEAM BUILDING THROUGH SELECTION

By aggressive recruiting and smart hiring, you can develop a higher quality team than your competitors. In order to select wisely, you must have the ability to discriminate between the abilities and personalities of people. Accurately discriminate between the right people and the unfit people. This fundamental responsibility is taken too lightly by everyone except possibly the president and vice president of human resources. By keen decision making, you can cut down turnover and attract those people who are going to make a real difference.

Having good people-judgment is a necessary skill for any executive, and most executives believe they are excellent judges of people. This is much less true than they think. Their judgment concerning people is not as accurate or as intuitive as they believe. Hiring the wrong person sucks energy out of you and the team.

The purpose of hiring is to gather experts around you. I once asked a highly successful restaurant entrepreneur who had 600 people working for him how he was so successful. He told me he had 600 experts working for him. Each food server was an expert in her section of the restaurant. Each busperson was an expert in his job function. Each hostess was an expert in the art of welcoming guests and making them feel great. Your role as an executive is to attract people who are capable of becoming experts in your organization. Experts respond to your vision and energy, and can help you collaborate and work on your vision and plan.

Create independence in your team. It is only through this independence that you grow beyond your self-imposed limitations. When you hire people whom you intuitively know you can dominate or who will be deferential to you, all you can rely on is your own intellect and energy, neither of which is as strong as you think. Weak executives hire people they subconsciously feel superior to. This is done as a protective device, and it has dramatic long-term consequences. Executives with a low level of self-confidence hire inferior people so they can feel superior. Slowly but surely, their division goes downhill. Often, these low-self-confidence executives change jobs before the deterioration is truly known or understood.

It is easy to gather around you a weak team. Hiring intellectually slow people and psychologically weak people doesn't turn out well for anybody. Don't look for sweet, gentle, kind people; they are inherently lazy. Select people who are intellectually driven and who want independence. Hire people who can grow in their jobs and take your place. When you don't recruit quality, you're a problemsolver. When you do recruit quality, you're a cheerleader. Hire people who are more capable than you in their expertise. Look for a sense of responsibility—the ones who blend head and heart. They don't need your help, but rather want your collaboration. They have little need for you and your energy, but a high need to combine their skills with your value system. *Independent* doesn't mean someone who works for their own selfish ends; independent means the employee works independently toward the group cause.

It's very easy to rush the hiring process—it requires tremendous patience to hire correctly for high-level positions. You want to hire somebody because it eases the anxiety of having the position open. Hiring a person represents a substantial investment. As in any investment decision, take your time. By being patient, you can even parcel out some of that open position's job duties and possibly provide job enrichment for someone within your organization.

I have found the following list of questions useful in the interview situation. Ask potential employees to answer them.

1. If you could make one suggestion to management in your last job, what would it have been?

2. What do you consider your strong points?
3. What do you consider your weak points?
4. What have you done about your weak points?
5. What accomplishments in life are you most proud of?
6. What has been the biggest disappointment in your career?
7. What is success from your perspective?
8. How high did you advance in your last job?
9. How high do you think you would have advanced if you'd stayed there, and why?
10. If I were to call your old bosses, how would they describe you and what would they say?
11. What outstanding example of tenacity is in your background?
12. How would you describe your management philosophy or style?
13. Why do you want this job as a career?
14. How much money do you think you're worth?
15. How hard do you work? What time did you arrive at the office this morning? Who do you know who works harder than you?
16. How would you describe the pace at which you work? Fast or slow?
17. Who are some of your heroes, and what causes them to be?
18. What would you like to be doing ultimately career-wise?
19. What do you want to do with your life aside from your career?
20. What is it that motivates you?
21. Describe a situation where you had a conflict with another individual and how you dealt with it.
22. What are your team-player qualities? Give examples.
23. What idea have you developed and implemented that was particularly creative or innovative?

24. Describe the project or situation that best demonstrated your analytical skills.
25. What is a team project of which you are particularly proud, and your contribution?
26. What types of situations put you under pressure, and how do you deal with pressure?
27. Tell me about a situation when you had to persuade another person to your point of view.
28. Knowing what you know now about your college experience, would you make the same decisions? What would change?
29. How would you react to having your credibility questioned?
30. How do you think you have changed personally over the last 10 years?

POWER TEAM TIPS

1. The executive is the magnetic center of the team's inner energy.
2. The executives' role is to model the behaviors they expect from their team.
3. The executive is in charge of translating the corporate vision for his team.
4. Conflict ultimately leads to higher-order truth.
5. Your team-management style is often subtly connected to the way you were raised by your parents and your family dynamics.
6. Your team is only as strong as the people you recruit and hire.

Chapter 6

Power Communication

All executives must promote themselves and what they believe in without fear. It is crucial to your career not to have "self-promotion reluctance." Self-promotion doesn't mean spouting off about all kinds of things you know little about, or constantly trying to impress your superiors with your intellect, dedication, or leadership ability. Nobody likes an insincere compliment giver. Most mature intuitive corporate executives see through this facade anyway.

You are generally treated and reacted to according to the signals you send out. A person like this plays to a superior person's ego needs, hoping to gain special privileges or favors. You'll see this tactic used with some success in your business career, but be assured that it can't, by its very nature, take you to the top. This is an *inferior* position. You don't become a top executive by assuming positions of weakness.

Remember, your standing on a personal level is generally a reflection of *your* self-esteem. If your voice changes into a high-pitched "Yes sir" or "Yes ma'am" when you're around upper management, if you show by your mannerisms that you wish to be regarded as a loyal and trustworthy servant of upper management, you will be given this role both hierarchically and psychologically. Many mid-level managers have told me "My number-one job is to make my boss look good." Upon first hearing, the statement is laudable. Loyalty, a quality seen less frequently than it should be, is respected and wanted in the corporate world. But what happens when you inevitably decide to focus on your own career? You're going against everybody's expectation of you, and will probably seem disloyal or selfish to those you once served.

Your number-one goal in your business career is self-promotion. And self-promotion is *not* selfishness, by the way. Self-promoters understand the needs of people because they are focused on others, not just on themselves. They accept the fact there are opportunities in life, and acknowledge to themselves that they are capable of filling those needs. Self-promotion is the filling of needs and placing in motion the energy of recognition and rewards you deserve.

There are limited opportunities in the corporate world, and there will never be enough top jobs for everyone who wants one. But there is nothing wrong with feeling deserving. In the business game, there is nothing wrong with believing in your inherent ability to handle people and being confident that your visualization of the future is correct. With a proper perspective, this is not an ego trip. Don't promote yourself only to see your name in lights. Other employees resent it when you sell your ideas primarily to promote your own ends. But if they see you benefiting the company, they tend to buy into your ideas. Of course this is especially true if they see their needs may be enhanced too. Do those things within the corporation that need doing; but have no fear about making sure your contributions are recognized. If you don't see that this is done, who will? You cannot be afraid to take on high visibility assignments; without them, you won't become visible.

My basketball coach once grabbed our low-scoring center at halftime, looked him straight in the eye, and asked him, "What's the first thing you think of when you touch the ball?" The center instinctively responded, "Pass!" "Dammit," the coach shouted, "That's why we're getting killed in the middle. Your first obligation when you touch the ball is to see if you are in a position to shoot! If we don't score more points than the other guys by the end of the game, we lose!"

The center was a good team player. He was humble by nature, and couldn't visualize himself as being a leading point maker. He saw himself as a defensive player who fed the ball to others. He was a much more talented offensive player than he gave himself credit for. By not acknowledging his abilities, and by defining his role as one of "making the other guys look good," he hurt not only his own chances for greater recognition and credit, but the team's chances of winning.

In the corporate world, as in a basketball game, when you're in the right position, shoot the ball! If you're afraid to shoot, then be a backup player. Executives with overly sensitive personalities are sometimes afraid to take on more difficult assignments that would distinguish them as leaders because they're uncomfortable dealing with conflict. They steer away from conflict because they're afraid of the many different emotions with which people could react. They are afraid that they won't conduct themselves properly, afraid of the power of their own emotions, afraid they won't be able to control them. They don't want to handle any tough issues, only those issues that are simple and straightforward, not those that are potentially rewarding or punishing. They don't bring up ideas for fear the idea will be rejected. So they sit back and become an observer of the action at group meetings instead of taking on a constructive leadership role. If you can't deal with conflict, or fear rejection, it's difficult to promote yourself.

There are many natural opportunities to promote yourself—simply riding up in the elevator, passing others in the hall, and so forth. If you don't make good eye contact, if your gaze averts downward, then you are seen as lacking confidence. When on the elevator with senior-level persons, look them in the eye and ask them how a tough assignment is going. Ask them if they need any help in handling it. Ask them to help *you* in some way, if this is appropriate. Don't be afraid to say *something*.

Say something meaningful like "John, I've noticed our sales are doing super in the northeast district. Why do you think that district is so impressive right now?" Or, "Sara, if you need somebody to explain what our department does to the trainees in orientation, I'd be happy to throw my name in the ring." Statements about how bad rush hour is now that they've closed Seventh Street or what a good deal you got on your new suit are trite. Don't bring up a problem, bring up a solution to a problem. Volunteer to do something beyond your job description.

There is no better way to promote yourself within the organization than by getting involved in the sales effort. This isn't always appropriate, but you should show no reluctance whatsoever to becoming involved with customers. Being involved with customers, especially big ones, is a coveted role. Bringing in the biggest deal of the year, or at least being involved in the effort, wins the respect of the entire company. If executives spent more of their time with customers instead of engaging in petty politics, corporations would run much better, be more enjoyable places to work, and have much better bottom lines.

COMMUNICATION SKILLS

Counseling psychology has identified the basics of effective communication. Present-day sales training is usually some version or derivative of communication theories and techniques which were developed originally for psychologists to use in dealing with clients. Counseling techniques have replaced sales techniques over the past two decades as the term *consultative sales* has come into vogue. Old-time sales training emphasized closing. Class participants would be instructed to ask for the sale at least five times. Obviously, times have changed. Society is more sophisticated. You can imagine what would happen if you sat down with the president or high-ranking executive of a company and asked for the sale five times! After the third blatant attempt, you would be trying to dislodge your brochure from your throat as you were politely shown the door with "If we're interested, we'll give you a call!"

You don't "hard-close" executives; you set the stage to allow their own free will to be in alignment with yours. The communication skills needed for this stage setting include using empathy to understand the other executive's needs and situation, using specific descriptive adjectives or words to correctly identify what they are thinking and feeling, being alert to facial or body language, and being able to understand what the person is *really* saying, not simply hearing what they are telling you. These skills I've so easily listed are as difficult as counseling skills to acquire and use effectively. But all executives need to learn these basics and consider effective communication crucial to their careers. They need to be lifelong students, always working to improve their abilities to listen effectively and communicate their thoughts.

There are several differences between internal promoton and external sales. The primary one, of course, is that people within the organization get to know you over time for who you really are, while in external sales there is usually—at least initially—some role-playing between parties. A backstabbing person's colleagues will eventually know and distrust him, but the same individual can be successful in promoting the company to the outside public, who only get to know the person superficially. Top salespeople are often despised internally because of their selfish, egotistical view of the world, while the outside world sees them as vivacious and charming individuals. Who is correct? Obviously the star has two sides: the social and the real.

As an executive, however, you cannot be seen as being temperamental or superficial. A consistent personality who demonstrates maturity day in and day out will consistently and effectively sell ideas within a company. The aggressive, obnoxious, high-producing salespeople get their way within the company on occasion, but they don't sell their position. They threaten to leave or make such an immature scene that the person of whom they are requesting the favor gives in.

When promoting your ideas internally, it is obviously much easier to obtain an audience with whomever you wish to communicate than to use a go-between. Half the battle in outside sales is getting an appointment with the decision-maker. Internally, for the most part, this difficult feat is not required.

Corporations have invested much time, effort, and resources in researching and understanding the sales cycle. The following techniques are as effective for selling your ideas as they are for selling products and services. Consider the following sales techniques whenever you are trying to influence someone in a one-on-one setting.

Establishing Rapport

In order to sell any idea or concept, it is important to set the stage so that the person you're dealing with or approaching wants to listen to you. It is initially disheartening to realize that your adrenaline runs ahead of their adrenaline; in other words, you want to be in their office more than they want you there! You have to work at making them want you in their office. Don't take this personally. Accept it as a communication fact of life.

Rapport is the first step of any meaningful communication process. *Rapport* is a harmonious relationship between people based on trust and understanding. The future of your interactions hinges on the success of your ability to create interpersonal harmony. It's your responsibility, not the person with whom you seek to establish rapport. If the two of you were at a cocktail party and you met at the beginning of the food line, both would have an equal responsibility to create a dialogue and exchange pleasantries. Neither of you would feel defensive or censor your statements, except to be socially appropriate. Defensive barriers would be down. Nobody's expecting the other person to say or do anything controversial. No one is trying to persuade anyone else to their point of view. The only interest is that the person in front of you doesn't take the last egg roll.

Initially, when you're trying to sell your idea, concept, or service, the other person will experience tension. She will keep her defensive barriers up until she feels she can trust you. Trust is what you're trying to achieve in a sales relationship. Our world moves very quickly, and trust requires time to develop. As the person in the selling position, it is frustrating that the other person reacts so slowly to our obviously (to us) good intentions. A useful truism to remember is, "The more genuine and open you are, the more the other person will perceive you as being trustworthy."

This involves what is known as the "mirroring" effect. People tend to mirror each other's behavior when they feel comfortable. When people sitting opposite each other feel comfortable, both will have their legs crossed or otherwise exhibit the same degree of relaxation. They both tend to smile to the same degree, and their voices are relaxed. The rapport phase implies that defensive barriers have been lowered and they are willing to talk openly about their situation.

The rapport phase continues until the other person feels relaxed. Initially, when you're trying to sell your idea, concept, or service, the other person will experience tension and keep his or her defensive barriers up until they feel they can trust you.

A PANOPLY OF DEFENSE BARRIERS

At the root of the lack of trust in an interpersonal encounter is the survival instinct. In a business setting, people are on their guard. They don't want anyone to take advantage of them. They don't want to disclose their thinking or perceptions about your proposal. They don't want to look stupid, or give away their position too early in the relationship. They don't want to be "sold."

The Desk

Most people believe that you're there to fulfill *your* needs, not theirs. The stronger this belief, the greater the intensity of their defensiveness. People will unconsciously or consciously put up barriers between the two of you. These barriers can even be physical. When we talk to fellow employees or customers, they may remain behind their desks. The desk acts as a shield from getting close personally. A more self-confident executive will get up from behind the desk and sit opposite you with nothing between the two of you. I have found this habit relatively rare, and upon the first encounter, most will stay behind their barrier. One little dictator I know has purposely raised his chair and had the two chairs in front of his desk lowered so as to make sure he can stare down at his visitors! I don't have to tell you how insecure this man is, or what it would be like to report to him!

Word Choosers

People may initially guard their words. An intuitive person can see them measuring and calculating what they're saying. There is a slight strain in the voice. There is a lack of relaxation. They choose their words quite carefully, and they immediately take the position that they don't need what you have to offer. This behavior is a reaction to the circumstance, not to you personally. Those executives with lower self-confidence, or who are overly sensitive, find sales distasteful because they personalize others' defensive barriers. They also do a much poorer job in gaining consensus among their fellow executives. They are only capable of running things as they have little persuasive ability, only the ability to direct. As I tell my executive sales trainees, if there were no defensive barriers, most everyone would be happy to go into sales. If somebody would set the appointment up for them and all they'd have to do would be to walk in, chat a bit, and have the other person sign on the dotted line to receive a big commission, most of us would volunteer for the role. We know this is not the case. People's defensive barriers cause them to be rude, unpleasant, discourteous, and at times just plain obnoxious.

Avoidance

People will refuse to talk to you or they won't return phone calls. I've found, by the way, that people who don't return phone calls are usually not as busy as they think. These people claim they are extremely busy and have little time to talk to vendors. Upon examination, however, it becomes apparent that much of their day is filled with control-oriented work: checking others' progress, reading somebody's action plan, attending unimportant meetings, and so forth. People who are too busy to return phone calls are generally poor executives who haven't delegated properly; hence, they are always "busy." Industry is catching on, however, and there is a definite trend to "flatten" the organization. Twenty people commonly report to one executive, instead of the norm a few years ago of seven or eight.

A variant of direct avoidance is the person who leaves his or her door open during your meeting. Seriousness implies the door should be closed; by leaving it open or taking phone calls, they are defending against getting close to you, letting you know that you come in second. You're never going to have an in-depth conversation due to these interruptions. Again, people who leave their door open or take phone calls during your meetings are poor executives. They lack self-esteem and have a need to demonstrate to *you* how busy or important they are, or they're trying to impress *others* in their organization that they're busy—or both. Any top-notch executives, once they've decided to see you, will pay utmost attention and give careful consideration to what you say; otherwise they're wasting their time. Many mid-level managers like to spend excessive time in the rapport phase, and interruptions are very much okay. After all, they're not going to make any decisions, anyway; they're simply looking busy by gathering data.

The Happy Face

When the other person is superfriendly, greets you with a big, happy grin, and agrees with everything you say, you can be assured he or she just likes to talk to vendors, and needs to be liked and admired. These people are generally very pleasant and cooperative, and except for their blatant superficiality, are enjoyable to be with. But they're wasting your time. They have no power within the corporation, and simply manage to fill a role until they get terminated. Don't worry, you'll see your old friend again when he or she calls you to see if you know of any job openings. After all, you're a buddy.

The Sourpuss

The opposite type of person, the ones who never crack a smile, are also using defense barriers to keep you at a safe distance. When you walk in, they glance at their watch somewhat obtrusively, and ask, "What have you got for me?" This type wants you to talk first so you can say something they conceptually disagree with, giving them a psychological excuse to dislike you or dismiss what you have to say. They want to push you out the door as quickly as they can. This type doesn't really listen to you. Most of the time, they're in a sour mood, and feel constantly under stress. They have virtually no capacity for empathy. This is not your big-picture executive, only a hard-working, somewhat inefficient stick-in-the-mud who really doesn't realize that this overly serious personality is a defense mechanism against expressing emotions. They are afraid of the power of emotion, so they keep a constant check on them, to the point of being boring.

COMMUNICATION TECHNIQUES

Empathy

Empathy is a word that's constantly used in management and sales training courses. Empathy is virtually impossible to achieve with another person. We can never *truly* understand what another person is thinking or feeling. But we can *try* to understand their view. The immature person's unconscious gets in the way, and they have a hard time viewing the world from another's perspective.

Some time back, the nightly news showed several hundred thousand Iraqi people screaming their lungs out to Allah about the terrible satanic United States, all the while beating themselves. I reflected that it would be extremely challenging to have empathy with these people on my TV. Their beliefs were so radically different from mine. Yet if I were trying to sell them *my* ideas, I'd have to take the time to educate myself about their society—what they believe and why.

Empathy is very challenging when it comes to understanding how different races perceive the world or how the opposite sex views the world. Nevertheless, empathy is essential to high-level executives. By being empathetic, we gain trust, and people's defensiveness is reduced. When people sense we are trying to understand *their* viewpoint, they are much more willing to listen to *us*.

Empathy involves self-discipline. You must be able to discipline your thoughts and emotions so as not to interfere with what you're being told. You resent the person who tries to put words in your mouth or tries to hard-sell their idea or position, don't you? Don't do it to others. The focus in creating rapport is to move from a no-trust to a trust position. The other person is asking himself or herself, on a subconscious level, "What are you trying to get out of this deal? How do you think you can help me? And what are your inner motives, anyway?" Again, all people we contact with a proposal or idea will initially have these thoughts. Don't take them personally.

Communicating with empathy is difficult, and professional counselors spend many hours in course work and laboratory studies trying to improve their ability to understand what another person is saying. They try not only to understand what the other person is saying, but put this understanding into words that the other person agrees with.

Empathy involves thinking of words that represent the other person's feelings, and using these words to tell the other individual that you are trying to understand their feelings and situation, and you're trying to place yourself in their perception of reality.

An example of an empathetic statement might be, "Steve, I can understand how disappointed you are that your deal fell through. I know that you were feeling optimistic." Often, we tell others, "I know what you mean," or "I understand," when we really do not. Keep your superficial statements down to a minimum. If you don't understand what they're talking about or feeling, politely ask them to explain it in different terms. They will be willing to do so.

Respect

Another building block of rapport is respect. *Respect* is honoring the other person because he's a member of the human race. Respect is developed when we try to understand the uniqueness and capabilities of others. Respect for others grows as we observe their efforts to try to live their lives successfully.

Respect is demonstrated. If, while talking to somebody, you're looking not at their eyes, but somewhere else, you're demonstrating a lack of respect.

When I first began my career, I came to work with a brand new doctoral degree. I felt very bright and gifted. A sales manager took me aside during my first week and said, "The first thing you have to learn about training our salespeople is that you must give them the respect they deserve. It takes a strong constitution to go out and knock on doors every day trying to develop business for this company. People who aren't in sales don't understand the psychological strength this takes. Respect our people for being able to do this. It is a rare person who can."

I haven't forgotten his words, and as a result of our conversation, I tried hard to respect the salespeople within our company. As an executive, respect your fellow human beings, respect all work. It is honorable—janitors and presidents are productive and move society ahead. A person's position within the company shouldn't determine the amount of respect you give her.

A company president I know elevates himself socially above his "worker bees." He constantly refers to the important people he knows and the chic places he's been. He was very surprised last year when he arrived at work to find his employees on strike and picketing. He had completely lost touch with them. He was too important to eat lunch with them, to speak to them in the hall, or to know them as people. By not having respect for his people, he destroyed what would have been an outstanding career. To this day, he doesn't understand what happened. "Those stupid people didn't know how good they had it."

Once I discussed this issue with a vice-president of operations who relished firing people. He honestly felt that through intimidation, instilling fear in others, and arousing conflict, he kept his people on their toes, alert, and producing more. He openly fostered competition between work groups. He felt this produced a better product. His erroneous thinking, which was an aspect of his authoritarian personality, eventually undid him. Common sense suggests that cooperation between work groups, not competition, is the key to quality products.

Be friendly, and care about your people. Have a moderate need to be liked. Don't have a high need to be liked or appreciated, nor a high need to be included, but rather a moderate need. This helps you balance the work groups' energies, and helps you maintain objectivity.

Early in my career, I approached a moderate-sized oil company to sell them my training services. Being young and somewhat compulsive, I arrived about 20 minutes early for my appointment. As I got out of my car, I noticed an older gentleman struggling with several large boxes, pulling them out of a van. It was a typical July day in Texas, and I had a choice to make. I could either walk by the old man and pretend I didn't notice his struggling, or I could take off my jacket and help him, get sweaty, and not look as good for my important appointment with the chairman.

I decided to go ahead and help. After all, I could repair the damage in the washroom, splash my face, and cool off before the appointment. I asked the older man if he needed some help. "Yes," he replied gratefully. Together we took them all out and put them in the lobby, where they were taken to another part of the building.

The older gentleman thanked me profusely and left. I went up for the appointment sweatier than I liked, but was surprised to be immediately ushered in to see the chairman. We sat down, and I began to go through my sales technique of determining needs and showing how my services could meet those needs.

A third of the way through, the chairman cut me off with, "Dr. Watts, anything you'd like to set up here would be fine. Please work with my senior vice president of human resources and set up your 10 training programs."

I replied, "Mr. Ford, you're not even sure of the type of training I'm selling."

He said, "I don't need to be sure. We need your type of attitude around here."

"What makes you say that?" I asked.

"The old man you helped downstairs was my father. If you'll do that, then you'll help my people have a better service attitude. That's what we really need. Regardless of what you're teaching them, I know that your personality and service attitude will come through in the training. That's what I'm after."

Genuineness

Genuineness refers to the ability to be real and honest with people. When you are perceived as not being genuine, people are able to reject you psychologically. Genuineness essentially means that what you say and demonstrate behaviorally is congruent with what you feel.

Be genuine without being blunt. On my career profile, I ask people to describe themselves. I have gotten this response from executives: "Too honest; other people can't handle my honesty." These executives are obnoxious. Their brutal directness is significantly impaired by their misperceptions of reality.

No communication skills course, or sales course, can substitute for an honest, straightforward personality. If you want to be a leader, you must possess some need to be liked by others. Without some need to be liked, you become ruthless and control-oriented. This type of executive is not wanted in corporate America. As always, the key is controlling your emotions and verbalizations. Be and act like who you really are. Genuineness is a lack of phoniness. Strive to be yourself, not who you think you need to be. The underlying aspect of genuineness is confidence.

Self-Disclosure

Self-disclosure is another communication building block. This is a frank, open, genuine statement of why we are in the other person's office and what our purpose is. We need to be direct in business and tell the person why we wish to meet with them, what we hope to accomplish, and what we are capable and not capable of doing.

The general effect of self-disclosure is to promote acceptance from the other person. Self-disclosure eliminates defensive behavior. When you sell your idea or proposal, all high-level business people realize that there is a benefit to you. There's nothing wrong with stating that this is the case.

People want some assurance regarding your intentions before they can trust you with information about themselves. Self-disclosure sets the tone for the meeting. When you disclose things about yourself and the prospect discloses things about herself, a mutual trust begins to develop.

When you self-disclose, you can talk about your perceptions of the situation. The other person often wants to deal with these issues, but is too embarrassed to raise them. When we withhold information that would bear on the other person's decisions, this is destructive to the essence of the relationship.

In order for people to do business with you, they need to know who you really are so they can relate to you more honestly. When you reveal some of yourself, your background, and your uniqueness, you begin to cement a relationship. Feel free and be spontaneous about your ideas, experiences, and feelings when they are relevant to the other person's interests or concerns and may impact his decision.

The revealing of self requires some risk-taking. Obviously, self-disclosure is not to say you should obnoxiously drone on about yourself, but when it is appropriate to the conversation, when it would help the sales process by helping the other person understand you, feel free to disclose something about yourself.

As a general rule, the rapport-establishing process should last only a minute or two if you already know the other person, and should last up to 10 or 15 minutes in business if it's your first visit together.

DETERMINING NEEDS AND MOTIVATORS

The second phase in influencing people positively to our position involves understanding what needs and motivators they have. These needs determine their value system and will influence their perception of our position. Needs predict motivators. Simply put, if a person has a need, we can safely assume that he will be motivated to fill it.

It seems almost trite to say that in order to sell effectively, you must be a good listener and observer of human behavior. In many respects, top salespeople and top executives are much more intuitive and understanding of people than psychologists are. Psychologists are used to being placed in a position where people are open and honest in expressing their feelings. This is not always the case, but when people are paying $100–150 an hour for counseling, they generally are pretty open!

This is not true in sales. To take counseling techniques and apply them wholeheartedly to the sales effort is a mistake. The top executive trying to sell his or her company must be a much more careful observer of human behavior.

Added to this is the fact that people are often unaware of their needs and motivations. They have a psychological need that they don't acknowledge to themselves: a need for admiration, a need for attention, a need for acknowledgment of their intelligence. Then, of course, they have their business needs, which may or may not include your product or service. When people are satisfied, they will not buy a change. Satisfied needs are not motivators. You must help people discover needs that are not satisfied, or which are in danger of future dissatisfaction. Help them to gain, or help them not to lose, and they will be more receptive to your ideas.

A former boss once told me that everybody is pleased with his secretary until he gets a good one. Then he realizes that he wasn't as satisfied as he thought he was; he just didn't know the quality he could expect. It's the same in selling your product or service. People may be satisfied with what they have only because they don't know the difference between what they have and what you offer. They may not understand the benefits. They may feel that what you're offering is not important, or that other needs are more pressing. They may simply not care, and figure that the problem you're describing belongs to someone else.

A skilled communicator has to have the ability to ask sensitive, open-ended questions. By asking open-ended questions, you are focusing the conversation by allowing the other person to talk openly and freely. Open-ended questions include what they like best or least about their current situation. What areas would they like to see better handled? What other people are involved who may have ideas about how to handle the situation? Which areas do they feel are adequate right now, and which can be improved on? How important is this idea to them?

These questions allow people to express their opinions about the situation. Listen carefully to what they're saying. A barometer of how effectively you're listening is your ability to summarize what they've told you before they move on to the next phase. If you can't summarize what the other person is saying in a succinct, direct way, you're not a skilled communicator. Practice the art of synthesizing and feeding back to the person what they've told you. Psychologists call this reflective listening, and it's an important skill to develop regardless of your position in a corporation.

By accurately reflecting back what they've told you, you ensure that you don't misunderstand, and it shows respect because you've listened so carefully to them you're able to repeat back what they've told you. Include in your summary their present situation, what their desires and wants are, and the obstacles they perceive as preventing them from obtaining what they want.

PRESENTING YOUR IDEAS

The next stage in selling your ideas is being able to present them attractively. If you've done a good job of lowering the person's defensive barriers during the rapport stage, and you understand which of their needs your ideas are addressing, you are ready to present your proposal. At this point, you know which features to highlight and emphasize—those that directly relate to the person's needs.

The other person is listening to you and will have three questions: How will your idea help me meet my needs? What is the cost, monetarily, psychologically, or timewise, to make this happen? Is your idea worth the cost?

When you present your ideas, direct your statement to answer each question sufficiently. This helps people buy into your proposal without feeling anxious. Remember the golden rule of business: if you were the customer, would you take the action you're recommending? By stressing benefits to the other person, it shows her how her life will be improved by buying into your idea. When you can answer yes to the golden rule of business, you come across genuinely because you're excited. You realize that the other person will benefit greatly by following your suggestions.

OVERCOMING OBJECTIONS

In all communication, it is helpful to learn to close the loop. In sales, this is called the *close*. In communication, we call it gaining commitment. In business, there must be action. In philosophical discussions, there is simply an exchange of ideas. Business can be philosophical, but it must be action-oriented to produce profits. All of your and the client's energy is wasted unless you can agree to do something. As the mature executive, you must take the responsibility to create the dynamics of action.

Be prepared to be direct and candid, and ask the other person if he or she will go along with your ideas or suggestions. If objections are raised, be prepared to address them. Don't be defensive if someone doesn't agree 100 percent with your idea or proposal. Again, empathy is the number-one ingredient for ensuring that you don't take the objections personally. People may fear taking action. They may not see enough value in your proposal or idea. They may not understand how your idea will meet their needs.

When people raise objections or disagree with you, this is, in essence, a positive sign. If they weren't interested or hadn't thought about your idea, they wouldn't care enough to raise an objection.

Objections often have two components. The first is the objection itself. For example, "I can't go along with this idea, John. I think it'll take too much of my time, and I need to pay attention to other aspects of production." Underneath is the second component, an objection that is not expressed. This thought may be, "I really don't want to go along with this proposal because you'll hog all the credit, and I'll end up doing all the work, just like the last time." The secondary reason is probably the real reason they're not taking action on your idea.

A professor of mine once told me there are two problems a counselor has to deal with: the one the client is telling you about, and the *real* one. People may not be aware of the real one themselves, and are only able to verbalize the one in their conscious awareness. The strong executive communicator is able to understand the other person's unconscious to a certain extent. A good communicator may have more insight into the person's unconscious than that person has. This is a sign of mature intuition.

The executive's job is to clarify and understand the real objections, and turn them into positive action. If you lose control of your emotions, or become angry or defensive, you lose your status. Learn to defuse objections, not overcome them. You defuse an objection by being patient, making sure you've understood the person's real concerns, and not becoming visibly emotional or upset.

The skilled executive is a skilled communicator. Without excellent communication skills, an executive is at a severe disadvantage. What an executive really does all day is motivate people, understand their needs, lead the team, and develop long-term strategies. All of these critical job tasks require excellent communication skills. Look at selling your ideas and yourself as a challenge for you to continually grow and develop.

POWER COMMUNICATION TIPS

1. Your standing on a personal level is a reflection of your self-esteem.

2. When you are in a position to make a difference, *act!*

3. Counseling psychology and consultative sales stem from the same theory—overcoming defenses, establishing empathy, respecting the other person, being genuine, self-disclosing to facilitate the other person's self-disclosures, determining what motivators the other person has, presenting your solutions to the person's needs and wants, gaining commitment, and overcoming reluctance to make a commitment.

4. The skilled executive is a skilled communicator.

Chapter 7

Power Vision

Executives are responsible for creating and establishing ideals for themselves and their teams. Each of us has a mental picture of the kind of person we could become if we were to manifest our finest qualities to their maximum potential. This setting of your personal ideal self is a necessary first step to maximize your potential. It's also an ongoing process. People who truly want to become better executives can and will. Form a basic belief and trust that, if you apply the right degree of energy with patience and resolve, the ideals you set will be accomplished.

Define your ideal by asking yourself probing questions that lead to a set of self-observations you know to be true. Become inspired by asking and answering the right set of questions. Unless the right questions are asked, efforts are one-pointed—often in the wrong direction. There exists a part of you that has the power to perceive yourself correctly. Through all the information and thoughts we process, we must answer our own questions with what is real and valid for us.

Questions to ask yourself could be:

What are my fears—the things that, if they occurred, would lead to unhappiness?

When I am my happiest, what am I doing?

Could I incorporate some of those dimensions of happiness into my job and career?

What is my management style—intellectual or emotional?

Could I find a better intellectual/emotional balance in my management style?

How can I more effectively lead my team to the extra bonus of synergy?

How can I give my energy to the team to create better cohesiveness?

How can I foster reciprocal interdependence among my people and between divisions?

Am I promoting myself effectively, or is fear keeping me from taking social and business risks?

EXAMPLE: A VISIONARY EXECUTIVE

Recently I had the pleasure of evaluating a mature young man (age 39) to be president of a large division of a corporation. Steve Townes was a particularly attractive candidate. A West Point graduate and an M.B.A., his career in the aerospace industry has been marked by success. At the time, he was senior vice president of marketing where he was credited with directing the effort to bring in $600 million worth of new contracts. He was considered one of the real leaders of the company, and both operations people and human resource people admired him.

It was not surprising for Steve to get a call from a well-known head-hunting firm to interview for a job as president of a division. The parent firm which had the opening asked me to assess Steve to see what I thought his chances would be to of making a good president.

Steve had flown to meet the chairman of the board of the holding company for an initial interview. Steve was impressed. The chairman and founder was an eloquent man of 65 years; the holding company's president was a young man of 40, only one year older than Steve. The chairman extolled the opportunities at his company to Steve—how he wanted independence and autonomy from his divisional presidents. He expounded about the great future of the company and about how he was looking for the talent necessary to reach the $2 billion mark in sales. Steve was enchanted.

I, in turn, was impressed with Steve. He wanted to know how he could improve himself as an executive and begin to prepare himself for a top job. Like all executives with confidence and a track record of success, Steve did not mind the evaluation process. He is the type who volunteers and looks forward to it. Steve felt that a complete executive assessment was a way to grow to his fullest potential.

Steve did especially well with both his interview and his testing. He displayed the skills discussed in Chapter 6—Power Communication—beautifully. He quietly and with subtlety took the leadership position in the interview. He was able to establish rapport with me easily. He began by giving me a sincere compliment about how he was looking forward to the evaluation to help him improve. He commented on how nice my office was and noticed that indeed the window did have a fine view. Immediately I felt a sense of genuineness and openness.

Because he felt comfortable and relaxed, I found I was being challenged professionally not to let the "halo effect" play too great a role. The halo effect is well known to professional interviewers; this happens when you are initially so attracted to somebody you are interviewing that you look for evidence to confirm your first impression and tend to discount any negative information.

Steve was free-flowing with his words and thoughts. He did not try to say carefully what he thought I wanted to hear, but said what be believed to be true. His eye contact was excellent. Steve didn't stare, but held his gaze steady. He showed respect to my office manager. When she came in to provide us with some coffee, he stood up and looked her in the eye and said a sincere thank you. After he left, she told me that she felt a sense of warmth and power in his presence.

Steve showed me respect too. After he finished a question, he would often ask me if I needed him to expand on any point. His responses to my questions showed he could easily self-disclose with candor and insight.

"What are your strong points?" I asked.

He replied, "I feel my strongest point has to do with character. I am forthright and believe in honesty and clean dealing with customers, vendors, and fellow employees. I also have a positive attitude; I have been disappointed at times when people fail to live up to their commitments, but I stay strongly positive because I know if I persevere, my goals and my company's goals will be reached. I have found that my sense of humor helps me to put life into perspective and not allow the daily stresses of life to affect me very much. I'm aggressive; I go toward my goals with a lot of energy. I also believe I have a good business head. I usually reach a deal with our customers that is fair to both parties. Loyalty is of paramount importance to me, and I believe I'm loyal to the people that deserve my loyalty."

When I asked about his weak points, his response showed astuteness and perception. "I'm an intense man, Dr. Watts. I am driven to be successful. Because of my intensity, I can make those around me tense. I want my people to enjoy their jobs, and I don't consider myself a tense person, but an *in*tense person. Unfortunately, people sometimes don't mirror my intensity, but instead appear more anxious in my presence. I feel that this may hurt the creativity and brainstorming capacity of my people at times. I also feel that despite my successes in business, I'm still naive occasionally. My West Point training can work against me. I forget that not all people were brought up to live by a code of honor. I have found most people in business to be honorable, but there are definitely some who aren't. Some more skepticism on my part would serve me well."

I felt his answers were thoughtful and showed good insight. Testing reflected what I had seen in the interview: a highly intelligent man (98th percentile) with a well-balanced, mature personality. He was an extrovert by nature, a man with strong passions. At one time in his life, he was ready to die for a cause he believed in—protecting America. This attitude still prevailed.

I agreed with Steve's disclosure his naiveté was a weakness. He believed people when they told him something. After all, he was a man of honor and tended to ascribe this trait to others too liberally. Our interview and testing ran a little overtime, and I decided to let Steve take some of the testing home, which I very rarely do. Applicants tend to cheat on any timed portion, giving themselves the liberal benefit of the doubt. Not Steve; when the time came to end the test he would put his pencil down as if I was there by his side—I knew this from this interview. Steve could look you straight in the eye and when he spoke, your intuition told you this man spoke truth.

The client company quickly offered him a job, *but he declined*. Yet the one thing he wanted most was a leadership position with a large company. I was intrigued by his decision, and talked to him at length about his reasons.

Steve, being an executive with vision, looked within himself for the truth of his situation and based his decision on that. He then sized up the parent corporation and read between the lines. Introspection led to intuition, which allowed him to separate truth from falsehood and illusions his ego wanted to believe.

After carefully considering his conversations with the chairman and president, Steve realized that their interview of him was not really an interview; it was a sales job. The chairman was a great salesman—he'd proved that many times over the years—but his company lived off and through him. Although the company was more than 20 years old, the chairman's transition to professional management never took place. The chairman did not have management skills, only sales skills.

Then Steve began to reflect on the fact that the president didn't really offer any opinions on his own, but only parroted on the chairman's cue. After Steve carefully considered their description, his intuition told him that the division presidents were really like big branch managers. Steve decided to confirm his intuition by calling various people in the industry to get their views on the parent company. Although people are sometimes understandably reluctant to talk, Steve got some facts.

Eleven of the 16 company presidents had left in the previous year and a half. About half had been fired; about half had quit. The parent company was strictly bottom-line-oriented. They were not willing to make capital investments; they needed the cash flow too much.

There was no loyalty from the top. As long as you made your numbers, you were fine; if you didn't, you were fired. There was little guidance or support. The chairman, his son, and the president were too busy looking for more companies to buy or negotiating to sell one of theirs. They came back to Steve with a sweetened offer that was tempting, but not tempting enough.

This type of corporation has to hire people who need a job. Most of the divisional company presidents are journeymen; they tend to change companies every couple of years. Like attracts like. They didn't give loyalty to anyone, and really didn't expect any in return. These types and the parent company made a good match.

And Steve made a good choice. Through knowing himself and his value system, he made the right decision. It won't be long before Steve gets a big break. In the meantime, he'll continue to make things happen.

THE POWER OF SELF-KNOWLEDGE

Chapter 1 challenged us to know ourselves as we are in reality—to see our true nature. When you become more aware of your true self, inner development begins. We often only want to believe the superficial, and convince ourselves that we have little need to change. Only through quiet reflection can the excitable nature of the mind be quieted; it is through quiet time that we discover where our goals for self improvement lie. Activity can then proceed at its fullest, and with accuracy.

Our choices and decisions sometimes seem like a maze of intricate and confusing paths with illusions thrown in to make finding the center even more difficult. The challenge of your consciousness is to find your own center.

I once heard an interview with a sculptor who had created the image of a beautiful horse from a large slab of marble. The interviewer asked, "What went through your mind when you sat down to work?" The sculptor replied, "I just looked at the marble and chipped away everything that wasn't a horse." When you look at yourself, chip away everything which is not pure truth. As you do that, the real you gradually emerges—your true identity, not an artificial, incomplete social facade.

We define executive success as both financial prosperity and emotional peace. Those who have not achieved executive success have failed to:

- Ask themselves the right questions.
- Consistently apply the necessary energy and discipline to maintain an achievement attitude.

Be determined to remain aware of your consciousness, don't deviate from your purpose, and keep working to reach your ideal self. When an intense application of will is wedded to a goal of value and truth, success is ensured.

How will you know when you're on the right track? When you feel intensely alive and have practical enthusiasm, you're exercising your will. When you have an urge or determination to obtain new knowledge and to improve yourself, your goal is one of value and truth. Strive to maintain steady, forward motion toward that goal.

With self-insight, you can accept your personal limitations and fully appreciate the challenges and rewards of using your strengths to capacity. The more you understand yourself, the more you understand others—and the less likely you are to blame others. By coming to know and realize your self—and your potential—you can reach the highest levels of wisdom and maturity.

GROWTH THROUGH MATURITY

Chapter 2 defined various aspects of the emotionally mature executive. This is the type of executive that business so desperately needs now. Even more will be needed in the future. Following are some general traits of a mature executive.

- Well-adjusted with a high self-regard.
- Healthy ego. Appreciates self, but doesn't indulge in self-aggrandizement.
- Feels compassion for the whole of humanity, not just certain social segments. Despite wide differences in life situation, natural gifts and liabilities, believes that all people have much in common. Believes that no one is master of his or her destiny, and that everyone experiences suffering.
- Tolerant. Respects the rights of others with compassion and humor.
- Thoughtful.
- Enjoys striving in his or her work. Enjoys accomplishment more than fulfilling survival instincts. Reaches

out to help others fulfill their potential and achieve job satisfaction. Helps others develop skills in both professional and personal lives.

- Sets goals at a high but achievable level. Takes the path of greatest resistance because that path is ultimately the most rewarding.
- Admires others. Doesn't mimic or idealize others, but finds positive traits and values to emulate.
- Doesn't think he or she knows it all already—is willing to learn from others.
- Realizes that luck is not nearly as important as the ability to apply talents over a period of time. Doesn't expect luck to substitute for competency.
- Deals with personnel problems directly, rather than keeping peace at any price. Believes that harmony in the workplace is an active goal requiring a proactive posture.
- Can delay gratification. Tries hard to break bad habits. Considers bad habits a sign of weakness.
- Sees difficulties as a normal part of life. Realizes that all people experience good times and bad times. Takes the bitter and sweet in life with resolution and courage, and continually grows as a result.
- Trusts others. Not gullible, but can delegate effectively. Doesn't overly worry about being taken advantage of.
- Gives credit to others; not a "credit hog." Has outgrown a high need for material possessions and has a desire to share credit. Can focus away from the personal self to the larger issues of the group.
- Maintains a detached attitude. Self-esteem is not dependent on business success or failure. Doesn't become ecstatic over positive results, or overly depressed about hopes that fail to materialize. When emotions run too hot, immerses self in another less-charged pursuit to regain a detached attitude.
- Seeks solitude in order to put life into perspective. Devotes at least 15 minutes each day to quiet reflection.

- Understands the power of silence. Recognizes the vital importance of tone of voice and choice of words.
- Thinks before talking. Sometimes exercises power in choosing not to speak.

INTUITIVE DECISION MAKING

Chapter 3 elucidated the concept that there are only two thinking processes: reason and intuition. Reason is secondary to intuition. We are taught reason in school, especially in an M.B.A. program. Intuition is a gift from our unconscious to use and profit by. Through reason we know the properties of things; through intuition we know the substance of things.

Properties are characteristics, attributes—a typical way for something to be or behave. Western psychology tends to study the properties of personality. For example, extroversion—the ability to be socially bold—is important in a manager and critical in a salesperson. Conscientiousness, the property of being dependable and responsible, is important in most occupations. The labels for these traits change over time and between labelers, but the substance never changes.

Substance is the essence of a phenomenon; that condensed, vital part that is the permanent cause underlying an outward form. And it is the substance of things which is most important. People will always describe properties differently. An executive must use intuition to recognize substance.

This need to recognize substance is what separates executives from managers. Managers execute policy. They must know the properties and responsibilities of their jobs to do this. Executives, on the other hand, set policy. Executives must understand the substance of themselves, their roles, and the jobs and abilities of the people under them, and then visualize the future. And we only understand substance through intuition.

Intuition is always providing us with information. But the ego keeps us from receiving this information, or distorts the information we receive, causing us to misinterpret it. A big ego is a weakness; the bigger your ego, the more you are controlled by it. Identify and call your ego a name, and then choose to put it in your back pocket so you can keep sitting on it! When your ego is controlled, and you can focus on the situation instead of your feelings about the situation, intuition is free to seep into your consciousness.

Intuition occurs in flashes. When you are not under the control of your ego or engaging in intellectual thought processes, your mind has the freedom to go where it needs to find solutions which are best for you.

Aspire to a set of goals that, if fulfilled, would make you happy. You must concentrate on the goals and exercise patience. Understand that there is a natural rhythm and cycle which events must go through. When an executive imposes an artificial deadline on results (for example, quarterly earnings) the company begins to focus on properties, not underlying substances. Your patience will be rewarded with greater intuition.

Most managers deal mostly with effects and rather blindly try to work their way through them. Strive to make your typical mood one of gracious peace, in which you can concentrate more fully. With this relaxed concentration, you can achieve illumination. By stilling the storm of your emotions, you think clearly and focus your energies consistently. Intuition helps you to discriminate between things that really matter and things that don't. Intuition is your sixth sense—truly the illumination of the mind.

ROLE AND STYLE

As Chapter 4 suggests, your leadership style is probably one of your greatest business decisions. Because no two personalities are alike, no two executives are alike. To help you recognize your style, we discuss two different basic approaches: executives who think and reason with their heads, and executives who think and reason with their hearts. No executive operates completely in one mode or the other, but one style usually predominates.

The heart executive looks for loyalty from his or her people. The head executive looks for performance. Both qualities are needed in an effective executive, and both must be developed equally. Executive effectiveness is a function of leadership qualities and appropriate responses to the demands of the situation. The executive's role is understanding how his or her qualities can benefit the situation. Try to see the underlying substance and enlighten the situation by defining it in a way that employees relate to and emotionally bond with. Employees give back to the executive loyalty and responsiveness to the vision.

When a dominant, intellectual executive demands compliance—either subtly or not so subtly—subordinates show compliance. But when the employees emotionally bond with the vision and feel they are part of the vision, they are truly self-motivated. The executive becomes a leader instead of a manager. The executive who dominates must continually exert pressure to achieve results. As time goes on, the employees build up a tolerance to the pressure, and more and more pressure is needed to achieve the same results. The executive who positively motivates uses his or her energy to start the process, and the employees lend their energy to furthering that vision instead of resisting or coping with it.

The heart executive leads with charisma. This ability is useful in times of crisis, when your people's motivational level can make or break a situation. The heart executive intuitively understands that all human beings struggle towards true expression. By allowing people the freedom to make mistakes and fail—a process that is abhorrent to the overly intellectual executive—your team's inherent, intrinsic motivation is stimulated. This motivation propels the organization in new, unexpected, exciting ways.

Head executives stimulate people intellectually. When a head executive is open-minded, creative solutions to complicated problems emerge. A closed mind leads to rigidity. Rigid thinking is an attempt at feeling secure. When a person knows something, there is a feeling of psychological security. Zealots with one-pointed tendencies all deeply believe their views are correct. We never knowingly believe something that isn't true. But our security is an illusion—it crumbles under stress. When wider possibilities are envisioned, the executive truly realizes the importance of all perspectives. This concept isn't something you can read to understand; it must be felt to be understood.

The executive's role is to help employees understand the company's vision. Companies are created to fill market niches and generate a profit, but they also exist to serve a higher social purpose and good. When people truly understand this higher purpose, they respond to their jobs with their superconscious—the highest and best use of the mind. Each department reflects the personality and culture of the individual that runs it. But the executive realizes there is a core of energy which permeates all. As a rock thrown in the middle of a pond creates ripples that encompass the whole pond, so the vision must be a pervasive feature of the whole organization. Companies fail because they experience confusion about their purpose and vision. Employees look to the executive and organizational structure to guide their motivation and energy.

DYNAMIC TEAM BUILDING

Chapter 5 examines the interrelation between executives and their teams. Mature executives realize the collective energies and creativity of a team are far greater than those of the individual. America was founded on the concept of individualism and individual initiative. The challenge of the visionary executive is to combine the entrepreneurial behavior and singular motivation of the individual with the collective synergy of the team.

Teams are made up of interdependent personnel who share responsibility for achieving goals. Before the 1980s, corporate America had few quality circles and employee involvement groups. As other countries began to outproduce America, we realized the value of the executive who can energize groups of people. A mature team leader sees cohesion as a function of intermember coordination, mission clarity, communication, problem solving, and the establishment of clear norms and roles for its members. The team leader again has the challenge of keeping the ego under control. In this way, the whole team's performance can be seen as one, and the entire team receives public recognition and praise for success.

The characteristics of a cohesive team are:

- Team members value being in the group. They will defend the group's purpose, qualities, and products against outside criticism or attack. Team members want to be accepted by the group and will alter their behavior accordingly. Members defend the group standards and norms and the qualifications for being allowed in the group. Teams will let new people know what norms of behavior are expected and will selectively reinforce and model those norms for new people.
- Members hold similar beliefs about the goals and purposes of the group. Members try to understand and validate other members.
- Members want and desire norms of expected behavior and are willing to live within these sets of expectancies. There is a tendency over the long run for behavior and attitudes to be consonant. In other words, if people say positive things about the group, they begin honestly to feel that way.
- Members recognize that secrets or deals made between members lead to mistrust and deception and tear away at the fabric of unity.
- Members try not to allow their emotions to be displayed negatively within the group setting and discuss individual differences behind closed doors. They

respect the fact that people come from different races, life experiences, and backgrounds, and respect those different perspectives. There is a tolerance for unusual people and different ideas. There is a willingness to compromise and admit fault if necessary. Quality teams do their best to eliminate prejudices and personal pride that destroy group consciousness.

- Members want to see others within the group succeed, and are willing to give their time and energy to help others fulfill their objectives. They are supportive of other members' efforts.
- Members realize that in order to maximize the stated and agreed-upon goals, they must participate. They don't withdraw their energy when they don't get their way. They are enthusiastic about the team's goals, and set goals at the ideal level. They take pride in the goals.
- Members perceive they can be successful if the team goals are met. They understand that the chain depends on all of the links for strength, and each of them is one of the links. Everyone on the team is important.
- Members understand the team's objectives and their roles in meeting those objectives. All people have their strengths and obligations to use those strengths to forward the production of the group.
- Members maintain open channels of communication. Everyone can talk to everyone else. There is not much emphasis on position or status as an indicator of an idea's merit. There is freedom to publicly discuss ideas. Teams experiment with ideas rather than prejudging on rational grounds or having a "we tried something like that and it didn't work" attitude. Everything gets a legitimate chance. People take risks and expect other members to take chances and occasionally fail.

WHY CAN'T SOME TEAMS ACHIEVE COHESIVENESS?

No single theory can account for how teams fail to develop, but researchers agree that if there is a general tendency of group members not to explicitly discuss the ongoing process (truth) with each other, cohesiveness diminishes. If people expect that honesty will lead to unpleasant or anxiety-arousing consequences, they keep their mouths shut. This creates conditions of social inertia, considered unresolved disputes. Such teams often self-destruct or fail to actualize their potential.

Cohesiveness fails to materialize when group members don't really respect each other. Being part of such a group is not desirable; it's a chore. Group members are not perceived as having particular knowledge or skill. Members merely act as if they hold a common set of beliefs. A function of the team leader is to draw out the talents of each member and publicly recognize them. This paves the way for members to respect each other's talents and contributions to the team goal.

THE ART OF SELF-PROMOTION

Chapter 6 deals with the fact that if you don't promote yourself, nobody else will. It is naive to expect to succeed with attitudes like "Good work speaks for itself," or "I don't like to toot my own horn." We all hate insincere chest beaters, but if we don't take the initiative to put ourselves in the position of being noticed, we have only ourselves to blame if we continually get overlooked for positions we want.

Visionary executives who can sell themselves are the ones who can find the balance between opposites. There is a balance in all of life. Seek the balance of inner harmony.

Be sociable • Seek solitude

Be passionate • Have an even temperament

Be accommodating • Enjoy meeting high individual challenges

Be exacting • Be flexible

Be spontaneous • Exercise restraint

Be realistic • Dream

Be trusting • Be questioning

Be fact-minded • Have imagination

Be forthright • Be diplomatic

Be self-assured • Be prudent

Be conservative • Be open-minded

Be team-spirited • Be self-directed

Be spontaneous • Be controlled

Be relaxed • Be energetic

Index

F

G

H

I

J

L

M

T

U

V

W

Also Available from Business One Irwin . . .

SURVIVE INFORMATION OVERLOAD
The 7 Best Ways to Manage Your Workload by Seeing the Big Picture
Kathryn Alesandrini
Survive the information onslaught and find the time you need to be more productive! Alesandrini gives you a step-by-step action plan to help you manage your workload without resorting to outdated time management practices.
ISBN: 1-55623-721-9

MAVERICKS!
How to Lead Your Staff to Think Like Einstein, Create Like Da Vinci, and Invent Like Edison
Donald W. Blohowiak
Liberate the boundless energy and creativity of your employees for more innovative, profitable ideas. You'll discover that you can encourage reluctant workers to get the most out of their jobs by giving more of themselves, build teamwork by treating everyone as unique individuals, and inspire loyalty by granting independence.
ISBN: 1-55623-624-7

EXECUTIVE TALENT
How to Identify and Develop the Best
Tom Potts and Arnold Sykes
Cultivate and grow internal executive resources for succession planning and corporate growth! Shows how to realize the full potential of every employee in the organization.
ISBN: 1-55623-754-5

SOLVING THE WORK/FAMILY PUZZLE
Bonnie Michaels and Elizabeth McCarty
Creatively solve the challenges facing you as you try to balance your professional and personal lives. Discover how to cope with guilt, communicate effectively, and organize your life to eliminate unnecessary stress.
ISBN: 1-55623-627-1

SAVVY BUSINESS TRAVEL
Management Tips from the Pros
Darryl Jenkins
Make your T&E stretch to its fullest potential! Shows individuals how to negotiate with airlines, hotels, and other vendors to secure the best rates.
ISBN: 1-55623-752-9

Available at fine bookstores and libraries.